CORPORATE SUCCESS THROUGH PEOPLE

CORPORATE SUCCESS THROUGH PEOPLE

Making International Labour Standards Work For You

Nikolai Rogovsky
and Emily Sims

INTERNATIONAL LABOUR OFFICE • GENEVA

Academic Foundation
NEW DELHI

This edition is published in India in 2006

by : ACADEMIC FOUNDATION
4772-73 / 23 Bharat Ram Road, (23, Ansari Road),
Darya Ganj, New Delhi - 110 002 (India).
Phones : 23245001 / 02 / 03 / 04.
Fax : +91-11-23245005.
E-mail : academic@vsnl.com
www.academicfoundation.com

Corporate Success through People:
Making International Labour Standards Work for You
(ILO); authors: Nikolai Rogovsky and Emily Sims

ISBN 81-7188-498-9

Printed and bound in India.

PREFACE

In a world of rapidly globalizing economies, enterprises face a dynamic business environment that requires them to be constantly competitive in order to survive and grow. At the same time, current economic realities (such as liberalization, globalization, continually changing customer demands, new structures of production and work) increase the importance of human and social capital for enterprise success. The competitiveness and viability – even survival – of enterprises increasingly depend on their ability to make employees motivated, skilled and committed. Such a task can only be achieved in a workplace environment characterized by a spirit of mutual trust and respect, non-discrimination, and good labour–management relations.

The Management and Corporate Citizenship (MCC) Programme, which is a part of the Employment Sector of the International Labour Office (ILO), helps build the management systems and managerial competences that enable enterprises to improve human and social capital and thus increase their competitiveness.

This book advocates and promotes the notion that the international labour standards (ILS) developed by the ILO are tools for good managerial practice, and that they reflect the principles upon which good management systems are based.

Corporate managers are in the front line in transforming management principles from an abstract vision into reality. In today's global economy, managers need to build their policies and practices on labour standards which are simple to understand, universally accepted, and take into consideration the constraints under which companies operate in competitive markets. The ILS are such standards.

The book seeks to help managers understand the interrelationship between best management practices and ILS by presenting numerous case studies from both large and small companies from different regions and industries. These case studies provide concrete examples of how to operationalize ILS in any enterprise, and demonstrate why doing so makes good business sense.

Göran Hultin
Executive Director
Employment Sector

CONTENTS

Boxes

ACKNOWLEDGEMENTS

The authors are most grateful to Peter Cappelli, Wharton Business School, as well as to Göran Hultin, Michael Henriques, Arturo Tolentino, Michael Urminsky and Jean-Claude Javillier of the ILO, for their extremely valuable contributions to this book.

They would also like to thank Irina Akimova, Charlotte Beauchamp, Barbara Cooper and Daniel Esser for their work on the manuscript.

INTRODUCTION

Is there a trade-off between treating employees well and succeeding in business? Many employers assume that treating employees well means higher labour costs and lower profits. But a number of companies have found that they can do well by their employees and also succeed in business. The aim of this book is to explain how. The evidence we present shows how social management practices can make organizations more successful. In many cases, they actually reduce labour costs; in others, increased labour productivity more than offsets the costs of improving the well-being of workers. Social management spans a range of issues, from hiring and recruiting to employee involvement and union relationships, and corresponds clearly to many of the basic principles enshrined in international labour standards.

Choosing to be a good employer

Employers can choose how to think about and manage their employees. Are workers merely economic inputs to the production process, to be marshalled when necessary and dismissed when no longer needed? Or are they more like partners, whose interests and abilities can be an important source of competitive advantage?

Good managerial policies and practices can engage the energy and intelligence of workers through the principle of reciprocity. Employees who are treated well by their employer will respond with efforts to help the employer. Employees who have a long-term stake in an organization, through job security, status, promotion prospects and financial interests associated with gain sharing, are more likely to be committed. Commitment in turn induces workers to act in ways that benefit the organization and its goals. The benefits from these policies go beyond avoiding the problems of an angry and withdrawn workforce. They include tapping the ideas and initiative of workers who are, after all, on the front line for improving work processes and business outcomes (Kogut and Zander, 1992; Coleman, 1989).

Employee-friendly management practices stress the importance of harmonious working relationships within an organization. These facilitate trust, which makes it easier for individuals to define collective goals and work towards them. Positive social relations can help promote organization goals.

Social relationships within firms can also facilitate the development of intellectual capital by making the internal transfer of knowledge easier. For example, we have long understood that workers advise each other about the best way to perform certain tasks; such advice is passed through social networks in the workplace. Studies have demonstrated that informal or tacit knowledge is crucial for organizational success and that positive social relations facilitate the transfer of that knowledge, while negative ones may actually block the transfer.

More and more firms are building their competitive advantage through employees. What makes some firms more successful than others is not just their technology or their current line of products and services, but their internal capabilities which determine whether they are good at a particular activity. The real competitive advantage of a company like Sony, for example, is not its current range of innovative products but its ability to keep on producing innovations. The key question is: what drives ability and innovation, sometimes known as "core competency"? In the present competitive environment, traditional advantages such as differential access to capital and customers are much more difficult to sustain in open markets. Superior products and services per se can easily be copied, and even patents generally offer only a temporary advantage over competitors.[1] The more likely reasons why some companies have greater capabilities and competencies lie in their organizational assets – the characteristics of the enterprise itself and how it operates. The most important of these characteristics relate to employees and the way they are managed.

Well-known and successful businessman Helmut Maucher epitomizes this view in discussing his business strategy (Maucher, 1992):

---

[1] Harvard scholar Ghemawat (1986) points out the following cross-industry findings:

- Competitors secure detailed information on 70 per cent of all new products within a year of their development.
- Patenting usually fails to deter imitation.
- New processes are even harder to protect than new products; 60 to 90 per cent of all innovations ultimately diffuse to competitors.
- Success may be harder to sustain.
- Of the businesses that have outperformed competitors in the recent past, few will be as successful in the coming decades.

> We businesspeople will be able, much more often than previously, to invest our funds wherever they have the best chance to be effective; to purchase, produce, and sell, to obtain funds and pay wages and taxes, in places where we feel the conditions are most favourable. Over the longer term, however, global competition will cause all of the artificially produced advantages of certain locations to disappear. What will remain are those advantages resulting from the availability of natural resources and – a central factor – from the human and professional qualifications of the work force.

In a recent Towers Perrin survey, 90 per cent of American high-level executives said employees were the most important variable in corporate success (Markowich, 1995). Many of them would say: "The best thing we can do for our competitors is hire poorly."

But will it be enough to recruit the best people on the market? Recent evidence suggests not.

Two sides of the human factor

When the dotcom sector was booming, bargaining power in this segment of the labour market shifted dramatically from employer to employee. As dotcom companies fought for recruits, winning the "war for talent" became one of the most important management functions. McKinsey & Co., a large global consulting firm, claimed that superior talent would be tomorrow's prime source of competitive advantage (Chambers et al., 1998). In the new economy, competition is global, capital is abundant, ideas are developed quickly and cheaply, and people are willing to change jobs often. In that kind of environment all that matters is talent. Talent wins (Fishman, 1998).

Professor Denis M.S. Lee, who studies hi-tech workers, observes that virtually all the management efforts with respect to information technology (IT) workers were directed at getting them in the door (Lee, 1999). Avron Barr and Shirley Tessler, who run the Software Industry Study at Stanford University, suggest that, at least in the leading companies, managers believe that the key to developing software competency is simply to bring in more capable employees, not necessarily to manage them better (Barr and Tessler, 1998). In other words, the only thing these companies were doing was recruiting; all other aspects of management, such as motivating the employees, organizing their work properly, and training them, were largely ignored. As a result, companies were often staffed with extremely high-quality professionals, but were not sure what to do with them. Moreover, when the technology sector slowed down, some companies realized that the employees they had were not necessarily the employees they needed. For example, some of these professionals had excellent technical skills, but lacked flexibility during sharp market downturns.

This example shows that high-quality human capital does not necessarily guarantee a competitive position and prosperity for a company. As Thomas Stewart (1997), a highly respected business author, puts it: "Most companies are filled with smarts, but (...) even the smartest people in the world need a mechanism to assemble, package, promote, and distribute the fruits of their thinking." This requires proper organization of their work. Says management guru Peter Drucker: "Only the organization can provide the basic continuity that (...) workers need in order to be effective. Only the organization can convert the specialized knowledge of (...) workers into performance" (Stewart, 1997).

Two other globally respected experts, Stanford Business School professors Charles O'Reilly and Jeffrey Pfeffer, share this point of view (O'Reilly and Pfeffer, 2000):

> Of course, companies that want to succeed need great people, and recruitment, selection, and retention are obviously important. But companies need something else that is even more important and often more difficult to obtain: cultures and systems in which these great people can actually use their talents, and even better, management practices that produce extraordinary results from almost everybody. The unfortunate mathematical fact is that only 10 per cent of the people are going to be in the top 10 per cent. So, companies have a choice. They can all chase the same supposed talent. Or, they can do something even more useful and much more difficult to copy – build an organization that helps make it possible for regular folks to perform as if they were in the top 10 per cent. (...) Hiring and retaining talent is great. Building a company that creates and uses talent is even better.

Thus, the human factor can be a valuable element in enterprise competitiveness only when it consists of two equally important aspects – high-quality human resources and good organization of people's work. The latter is often known as human resource management (HRM). In practice, this means that it is not enough to recruit the best, it is equally important to make the best use of that talent. Managers have to:

- design the workplace and draw up the work schedule;
- provide training for the skills that talented people may not possess (e.g., interpersonal or leadership skills);
- motivate them;
- monitor their performance;
- make sure that their work environment is safe;
- make sure that no one is discriminated against;
- make sure that their voices are heard.

Many observers believe that the quality of human resource management is more important than the quality of human resources per se. Percy Barnevik of ABB suggests that long-term competitive advantage can be achieved only through excellent organizational structures and processes. Leif Edvinsson, Director of the Intellectual Capital unit at the Swedish firm Skandia AFS, suggests that "structural capital is more important than human capital". Sports fans will probably agree that a disciplined team without high talent is always better than a team that consists of unmotivated, disorganized and uncommitted superstars.

Of course, the higher the quality of employees, the better. But this is not enough! You must understand what you want from them, how to motivate them, where and how you will be using them, and where they can contribute most effectively to your organization. This is not easy. However, companies can learn to manage better through benchmarking against the innovative and effective labour practices of other companies and international labour standards. This publication aims to help executives design effective policies and practices for labour and social management in their enterprises.

We would like to stress that the points we will be talking about make sense only if you try them out yourself, in your organization, your company, your team. Consider this saying of Confucius.

> I hear and I forget
>
> I see and I remember
>
> I do and I understand

The aim of this publication is not only to indicate the problems that managers might face. Using examples from different industries and from all over the world, we attempt to show *how* things can be done. Lew Platt, former CEO of Hewlett-Packard, emphasizes: "Execution is what spells the difference between success and failure" (Linden and Upbin, 1996). Larry Bossidy, former CEO of Allied-Signal, echoes this view: "The competitive difference is not in deciding what to do, but in how to do it. Execution becomes paramount" (Stewart, 1992).

The examples of best management practice discussed in this book build upon the international labour standards (ILS) adopted by the International Labour Organization (ILO). A brief introduction to the ILO is provided below to help you better understand the principles behind a people-centred business strategy.

The ILO – What can it do to help?

The idea of international standards for labour came in part from the business community at the beginning of the twentieth century. Successful entrepreneurs wanted to develop an international framework that would allow conscientious employers to improve the quality of life for their workers and still be competitive. The ILO was formally established in 1919 under the Treaty of Versailles.

The ILO is a tripartite organization. This means that all decisions are made by representatives of governments, employers and workers. Consequently, a "reality check" is built into international labour standards. From its inception the ILO recognized the importance of creating win-win strategies for workers and employers, as well as for society as a whole.

The ILO works to promote equality of treatment, social justice, and improved working and living conditions for all. It does this through:

- ILS, which are benchmarks for good governance in both the public and private sectors;
- technical assistance to help governments implement ILS; and
- education and promotional activities to raise awareness and understanding of ILS.

ILS cover a broad range of topics. In this book, we have selected those that are particularly relevant to managers, based on the provisions of the most up-to-date standards.

ILS come mainly in two forms: Conventions and Recommendations. Conventions are legally binding on member States that ratify them, while Recommendations are intended simply as guidelines. Conventions and Recommendations are supplemented by other documents which set out very general principles and values that all States should follow, and codes of practice for areas such as occupational health and safety which are highly technical and change rapidly with new scientific information.

Almost all ILS directly address only the actions of States, not workers or employers, since generally only States are the subject of international law.[2] But ILS implicitly require or recommend action on the part of employers. For example, most ILS set out only general principles; therefore, governments usually need to consult employers' associations and workers' organizations on the details. Employers then have an implicit obligation to assume an active role in working with government to achieve the goals set out in ILS,[3] by:

- providing the government with information to improve policy-making and legislation;

[2] However, the ILO adopted the Tripartite Declaration of Principles concerning Multinational Enterprises and Social Policy in 1977, which was updated in 2000. This document affirms the importance of multinationals adhering to basic ILS, regardless of where production takes place.

[3] Since the detailed implementation of ILS will vary between countries, what is actually required of managers in a particular country may well exceed the basic provisions described in footnote 4.

- providing information to workers; and
- working with unions and other workers' organizations in a spirit of cooperation.

Although ILS do not address managers directly, the principles underlying the standards can add a new dimension to management philosophy, policies and practices. The enterprise values described in this book mirror the values upon which ILS are based – treating workers with dignity and respect, trust and fairness. At the same time, the ILS are globally accepted principles, supported by governments, employers and workers from almost all countries of the world. Therefore, they can help companies to transcend country- and culture-specific values. Multinationals might consider ILS as guidelines for the values that a company should uphold, no matter which country or region it is dealing with. Verifiable adherence to fundamental ILS[4] may help managers in developing countries promote their goods and services in international markets, and also help them create partnerships with multinational enterprises (MNEs). ILS can also help managers understand the expectations of international markets, since civil society activists often use ILS as a benchmark in assessing whether companies are socially responsible or deserve to be boycotted.

The following chapters will explain how labour standards can help enterprises carry out the different functions of social management. First, we take a brief look at some companies which have implemented social management systems.

[4] The fundamental ILO Conventions set out minimum standards for eliminating forced labour, discrimination, and the worst forms of child labour, for restricting other forms of child labour, and for promoting freedom of association and collective bargaining.

SOCIAL MANAGEMENT IN ACTION 1

What exactly does it mean to invest in social capital, and how can this improve business performance? The following cases offer concrete examples of people-oriented policies in action. They include an American high-tech company, a Bangladeshi textiles manufacturer, and a European sports shoe MNE with suppliers in East Asia.

Case 1. SAS Institute: A company of the future?

SAS Institute is a world leader in the software industry. Its annual revenues grew from US$98 million in 1986 to US$871 million in 1998 (O'Reilly and Pfeffer, 2000). But what really makes it different from the competitors is its staff turnover rate of only 3 per cent, while average turnover in software is estimated conservatively at more than 20 per cent. The 17 per cent difference multiplied by the size of the workforce means that SAS loses about 925 fewer people per year than other comparable software companies. With replacement costs at one to two times the annual salary, even conservative estimates suggest that SAS Institute is saving more than US$100 million per year from its lower turnover, almost one eighth of its revenue! Lower turnover also helps build and maintain customer relationships. "In a company with high turnover, (…) customers soon come to believe they are providing on-the-job training, a comment we often hear about accounting and law firms. It is not a model designed to build customer loyalty" (ibid.).

So, why do people stay at SAS? Salaries there are the industry average, and a lot of people actually take pay cuts to work for them. The company does not provide employees with stock options, phantom stock, performance shares, or similar schemes. People stay because they are attracted by SAS values and management ethics. The SAS philosophy is based on four principles:

1. *All people at SAS Institute are treated fairly and equally.* SAS emphasizes egalitarianism. It has a very flat organizational structure; depending on the particular division, there are only three or four levels in the company. Everybody at SAS (including assistants) has a private office, not a cubicle. Nobody, including SAS co-founder, Dr. James Goodnight, has a reserved parking space. There is no executive dining room. Everybody has the same health plan.
2. *People should be treated with respect and dignity.* SAS Institute believes in the power of reciprocity – if you treat your people well, they will treat the company well by being loyal and dedicated in return. SAS does not create a 'periphery' workforce by outsourcing. Day-care workers, on-site health professionals, food service workers, even security guards are all SAS Institute employees. SAS is making extensive efforts to signal to employees that "it sees them as human beings, not just workers" (Prusak and Cohen, 2001).
3. *SAS believes in and relies on intrinsic, internal motivation.* Management trusts people, treats them like responsible adults and relies on them to do a good job. SAS has no formal sick days or sick leave policy; if people are sick, they simply stay at home. Performance appraisal forms have been eliminated. Instead of formal appraisals, managers spend time talking to their people and providing feedback on a regular basis (at least three times a year).
4. *A good work-family environment pays off.* Company headquarters consists of buildings scattered over a 200-acre campus-like setting with a lake, beautiful grounds and forests. Company policy is for people to work about 35 hours a week; if you call after 5 p.m. the voice mail system tells you that the company is closed. This policy is based on the assumption that people do not perform effectively when they are tired. Dr. Goodnight comments: "I've seen some of the code that people produce after these long nights and it's garbage. (…) I'd rather have sharp, focused people that write good code that doesn't need as much testing. (…) Company X has three testers for every programmer" (ibid.). The reduced work hours help people to balance work and family commitments. Employees do not have to give up their careers if they want to see their children – as a result, more than half of SAS managers are women. SAS has an on-site medical facility with an average waiting time of five minutes. The company even helps with housing: it sells some of the land it owns to employees at discount prices so they can build homes. Some observers describe the SAS campus as akin to a giant plantation (Cappelli, forthcoming).

SAS Institute is a successful company, and its success could be explained largely by its values and the management practices that follow from these values. SAS shows that even in an era of relentless pressure, a company can differentiate itself from the competition and succeed just by being nice to its people. Is it an anachronism or an enterprise model for the twenty-first century?

SAS Institute operates in an industry with relatively high profit margins, but companies in markets with much slimmer margins can also create a people-centred climate for their employees, as our next case shows.

Case 2. BANTAI Industries: People-centred policies in the textiles industry[5]

BANTAI Industries Private Limited is a Bangladeshi company that manufactures baseball caps for the American market at its factory in Kalyanpur, Dhaka. Twelve production line supervisors oversee 370 machine operators and operator assistants. Ninety-two per cent of the employees are women.

The CEO of the company, Mr. Muhammad Saidur Rahman, has over two decades of experience working for relief and development agencies in Bangladesh, including the Red Cross and Oxfam. Mr. Saidur and his management team believe that the basic rights of workers to a safe and healthy work environment, as well as a fair wage and freedom from exploitation, are as important as corporate productivity and profitability. They also believe business should take responsibility for providing social services for workers, such as basic health care and family planning, and education for children. BANTAI emphasizes human empowerment and the right of all people to fulfil their potential. It creates a workforce with high self-esteem.

Most BANTAI workers come from rural areas. In order to prevent accidents, these young women are given several days' orientation in the use of sewing machines before they start their in-house training programme. A female doctor from Dhaka Community Hospital visits the factory at least once a week to provide treatment, guidance and advice to the workers. An NGO called Concerned Women for Family Planning provides advice and contraception. There is a day-care centre for infants and a non-formal primary school for 90 children. Through discussion meetings and individual counselling, BANTAI raises workers' awareness of important social issues affecting women such as dowry, marriage and divorce.

[5] Source: Choudhury, 2001.

BANTAI is a successful company, and its management believes that increased productivity and profitability is due to the company's welfare and social development programmes. Staff turnover is very low, and absenteeism is less than 1 per cent. The workers have a sense of full participation, ownership and organizational commitment. There has never been a strike, unrest or agitation in the company since it was formed in 1990. Product quality is exceptionally high, with a rejection rate of less than 0.15 per cent, compared with the industry average of 2.5 per cent.

BANTAI and its workers are doing their best to sustain their success. But they want to do more. They feel that as a member of society they have to promote their experience and corporate values. BANTAI management is trying to promote people-oriented practices, including women's health practices, within the country's business community. Mr. Saidur was able to convince managers to follow BANTAI's example by providing evidence to support the business case for social management programmes. There are now 40 to 50 factories with health programmes and about 20 factories with day-care centres in Bangladesh. BANTAI is also promoting its success through national television and the press, and Mr. Saidur is sharing his experience in international conferences and workshops. One such conference, held in Dhaka in May 2000, was attended by 70 garment factory owners and managers, as well as representatives from MNEs such as Nike, Reebok and Sears. After Mr. Saidur's presentation, some MNEs expressed their willingness to have their subcontractors replicate many BANTAI practices, and during this workshop the Social Standards Working Group was established by 12 companies to share ideas and experience in social management. Mr. Saidur currently coordinates the group, and one of its first tasks was the publication of *Guidelines for Welfare and Development Programmes for Factory Workers*. The publication was co-financed by the ILO.

BANTAI's management approach has had a positive impact not only on the firm and its employees, but also in defining the standard for others to follow. Our last case illustrates how a company can take proactive measures to ensure that its suppliers follow people-centred policies.

Case 3. Adidas: Social management and business success

Adidas is one of the top three MNEs producing sports footwear. It sources a large percentage of its products from factories in developing countries where, until recently, working conditions have generally escaped criticism. However, since the mid-1990s, Adidas has been paying close attention to issues such as working hours, health and safety of workers, working environment, and freedom of association. To a large extent, this move was driven by the growing concerns of consumers and the mass media in the United States and European countries about working conditions in this industry.

Like most of its competitors, Adidas was facing increasing public pressure to impose higher labour standards on its suppliers in developing countries. Some MNEs took a reactive approach, simply defending themselves from outside criticism and viewing social management as an inevitable money-losing part of the organizational activities. Adidas, however, decided to take a hard look at its management practices to see if they should be adjusted to the reality of today's world. As a result of this exercise, Adidas concluded that social management should become a part of its mainstream business strategy. Moreover, the company realized that worker-oriented policies and practices, aimed not only at Adidas employees but also at the employees of Adidas suppliers, could benefit the organization. Adidas introduced a system of labour standards, known as SOE (Standards of Excellence), which was gradually integrated into all the major components of the company's management system.

At the same time, growing international competition pushed Adidas to look for new ways to operate. As a result, the company launched a new production system, based on Total Quality Management (TQM) principles, that was expected to help improve productivity and increase output.

Improving labour standards was crucial to implementing this new approach. For example, one of the principles of the new production system adopted by Adidas is to allow workers to stop the line if they feel that this is necessary, giving workers the right to make honest mistakes. Workers are also better protected from the risk of injury due to their knowledge of health and safety standards. And they are better rested due to the limits imposed on their hours of work.

In 1999/2000 Adidas performed a pilot test in Asia, introducing the new production system at some suppliers' factories. Adidas had expected to spend up to a year introducing the new production system, but successful results were achieved after only six months due to labour–management partnerships in the factories, and a beneficial combination of vocational training and training in labour standards.

As a result of this pilot test:

- employee turnover went down, in some cases by 50 per cent;
- a cleaner and safer work environment was created;
- productivity went up by 100 per cent.

As one of the top Adidas managers puts it: "Compliance with labour standards is investment in people to make manufacturing successful. Labour standards and TQM principles send the same message: workers and their opinions are important. From top-down to bottom-up – that is the most fundamental change."

The Adidas case shows how enterprise policies and practices which emphasize social management can facilitate improvements in work organization.

SAS, BANTAI and Adidas are very different in terms of industry, geographical location, size and many other variables. What do they have in common? They are all building their competitive advantage on a people-centred management philosophy that emphasizes trust, treating people with fairness, respect and dignity. Such a philosophy is translated into a whole range of social management policies and practices, beneficial for both employees and enterprises. In the following chapters we examine particular aspects of people-centred management practices in more detail and see how international labour standards can help companies develop social management principles.

ATTRACTING HIGH-QUALITY WORKERS

2

New approaches to recruitment and selection, including online recruiting, are crucial to a company's competitive advantage; this fact demonstrates the growing strategic importance of people. Recruitment is becoming much more than just a function of the HR department. Peter Cappelli explains:

> Labour statistics reported last year that "corporate recruiter" was the hottest job in the labour market. Online recruiting is (...) changing the status of recruiting within companies and, in the process, helping to redefine human resources. Recruiting has become much more like a sales function, in contrast to the rest of human resources, which is a much more deliberative and reaction function. (...) Many companies have moved the recruiting function into its own area. Recruiting at Cabletron's Global Technology, for example, now reports to business development where the culture and pace of work are more similar and entrepreneurial. It has peer relations with the human resource function. (Cappelli, 2000.)

Particularly in countries and regions where unemployment is high, many employers pay little attention to selecting their workforce because they see it as simple matter: there is no problem finding enough people to get the work done. The complication is that some workers fit a particular job much better than others, and studies increasingly confirm what most line managers already know – that the most suitable employees are worth considerably more than the average. Finding and keeping them is the problem. Even in countries with massive unemployment rates, employers report difficulty in finding workers with the ideal profile.

Despite the growing realization of the importance of hiring the best people for a competitive edge, the majority of companies still fail to see recruitment and selection as important tasks that are worth developing. Most organizations, for example, simply wait to see who applies and then look only briefly at an applicant's credentials before making a hiring decision. For white-collar jobs, they then make a selection based on interview, despite the well-documented fact that interviews are about the worst method for determining which candidates will make good employees. Perceptions of applicant ability based on the typical method of unstructured interviews, where candidates go from one person to another for open-ended conversations, have practically no correlation with subsequent performance in jobs. Many employers appear to have no systematic arrangements for selecting among applicants.

The irony here is that there is nothing particularly difficult about developing a competency at recruiting and selecting employees. The principles are well-known. They begin with the common-sense notion that applicants differ in their abilities, they make choices about where to apply for jobs, and you want the most suitable people to apply to work for your organization. How applicants make that decision is the issue. That decision starts with the reputation of your company. The best candidates know that their prospects are good (even if it may take some time to find a good job), and they won't apply for a job at a company with a reputation for treating employees poorly because they think they can do better.

Since a lot of people nowadays search for jobs through the Internet,[6] more and more companies are trying to build their reputation through their website. As Cappelli points out (Cappelli, 2000):

> At the company's website, savvy companies work hard to help develop a positive "brand" associated with working for their company. They list all their workplace awards, such as the Working Women's 100 Best Companies, right on their home page. GE Power Systems highlights links to information about diversity, employee benefits, and work and family balance on its page. Booz-Allen, Hamilton lets applicants see what a consulting engagement is like, in this case a pro bono engagement to help the Special Olympics, which also demonstrates the company's community-oriented values. The aspect of online recruiting that could use the most marketing help – and appears to be getting it – is writing more interesting job applications, a task that many companies have moved from the human resource department to the marketing department.

Having a good reputation as an employer does not mean that a firm is an easy or soft place to work. In fact, one of the worst situations for recruiting is to have a reputation as a company that doesn't require much from workers, because this is more likely to attract workers who demand little from themselves. A firm needs a reputation for offering the best opportunities to workers who are highly capable and willing to work hard.

One way to help attract the right kind of applicant is to give potential candidates an accurate impression of what the company is like. This can be done through "realistic job previews", which provide a truly representative

[6] The Internet is an increasingly popular way of searching for a job in developing countries. For example, the majority of young professionals in Moscow are using the Internet as a major tool of the job search (author's interviews with MBA students at the Academy of National Economy in Moscow, December 2000). Some countries, such as China and Thailand, have begun providing Internet access to jobseekers as part of their public employment services.

picture of what it is like to work in a particular job. Many employers think they should paint the most favourable picture of the job, whether it is accurate or not, in order to get the best people to apply. They hide the problems and the difficult aspects of work because if applicants see them, they may not apply. The problem with this view is that attracting the best applicants is not the end of the process. Employees who find that the job is not what they expected will quit, and the costs of this kind of turnover can be enormous.

Studies of the recruiting process increasingly confirm the old wisdom that a firm's employees are its best means of promoting its reputation and obtaining good applicants. Employees know what is required, sometimes more accurately than management does. Current employees often know people who are good workers with the right attitudes and skills to make good colleagues. And they have an incentive not to refer bad candidates because they do not want to be the source of problems if a bad worker is hired on their recommendation, or to be drawn into conflicts at work. In addition to the fact that personal recommendations tend to be better-quality applicants, they also do better on the job, partly because the workers who refer them help them learn. This relationship means, of course, that it helps to have the best workers doing the referrals. It also means that any effort to present an unrealistic preview of a job will undermine the system because applicants will quickly see the difference between what the company says and what its existing employees say.

Getting a good pool of applicants is only the first step in securing a good workforce. The next step is selecting from them. As noted above, few employers make much effort to select among applicants, but even some of the more complicated methods are not very accurate. Selection tests are generally limited to predicting performance in the entry-level job. The best of these tests correlate at levels under 50 per cent with actual performance and most predict far less (even a 50 per cent correlation translates into predicting only 25 per cent of the variation in performance). But that still represents an enormous improvement over chance.

Research on the benefits of diversity in organizations shows a complex picture. Diversity in the composition of the workforce based on age, gender, or race can create conflict if employees hold strong prejudices. However, such obstacles are not insurmountable if workers are given sensitivity training and encouraged to work in diverse teams to overcome their prejudices. Furthermore, research shows that diversity can improve workgroup performance in many tasks because it brings a wide range of information, resources, and decision-making approaches that lead to better outcomes (Williams and O'Reilly, in Staw and Sutton, 1998). The extent to which a more diverse workforce improves the performance of workgroups no doubt differs by task.

However, as an executive from Xerox put it: "Managing diversity = managing for productivity" (Ferris, Rosen and Barnum, 1995).

Many employers have begun to take proactive measures to diversify their workforce, whether in response to legal requirements or on their own initiative. They have begun to give preference, other things being equal, to applicants from groups that have traditionally suffered from discrimination, such as ethnic groups, women or older workers. Critics believe this means that less qualified workers will be hired or promoted. The evidence suggests otherwise. A recent and important survey of empirical research into proactive measures in the United States drew several noteworthy conclusions (Holzer and Neumark, 2000). First, organizations that take proactive measures are effective in increasing employment and participation among the target groups. Second, employers who fight against discrimination seem to recruit and select more carefully, that is, they look at a broader pool of applicants and evaluate them against a wider range of criteria. Finally and most importantly, these employers do not appear to lose out in terms of employee performance. In fact, the job performance of women and minorities hired by these employers is, if anything, higher than the performance of white males. Through more careful recruiting, proactive employers seem to uncover attributes in women and minorities that are associated with better job performance. As noted earlier, most employers do not use sophisticated techniques for screening and evaluating applicants, and the results are not very accurate, whereas employers who strive to diversify their staff typically develop better methods of selecting workers, which leads to better performance.

The following case from the Philippines shows how actively recruiting people from groups that have suffered discrimination in the past can strengthen the company's relationship with the community and help with recruitment and retention.

Case 1. Yazaki-Torres Manufacturing, Inc. (YTMI): Equal opportunity as a core management strategy

Around the mid-1980s, customers in the world market for automotive gauges and PVC electrical tapes started noticing Yazaki-Torres Manufacturing, Inc., based in the Philippines. By then, it had developed a strong reputation for capability and strict adherence to quality. The 1980s saw a sevenfold plant expansion leading to more productivity and awards of excellence from the government and the business community in the Philippines and from recognized trade groups and customers abroad. The company was recognized for its high standard corporate leadership, management systems, quality production systems, employment and labour relations and community relations.

From the very beginning, Yazaki-Torres saw the need to invest in its internal customers, its people, and the culture of its organization. Management refused to leave anything to chance. The president of the company has always believed that the key to success is treating its workforce as its number one asset.

In June 2001, Yazaki-Torres employed 5,508 people. Eighty-five employees (1.5 per cent of the total workforce) were supervisors, managers and directors, while 5,423 (98.5 per cent) were rank-and-file workers.

Management saw the need for good relations with the surrounding communities to ensure a steady supply of skilled and trustworthy workers from the locality, and to protect company property, people and operations from theft, destruction and harassment.

Since it was founded in the early 1970s, Yazaki-Torres has gone a long way towards perfecting itself as an equal opportunity company. It has regularly instituted measures to affirm the worth of individuals who are traditionally discriminated against in the domestic labour markets. These measures benefit not only the existing workforce, but also those who have worked for YTMI in the past, and those who may work there in future.

Over the years YTMI has developed strong and close relations with its five host municipalities. Whenever the company needs to hire new workers, inexperienced local youth from these municipalities are given priority through referrals from the community leaders.

Yazaki-Torres considers hiring to be the starting point of a continuing relation with customers, as quality service is dependent on the quality consciousness and work discipline of each employee. Given the technical nature of its production, the company generally requires high school graduates for its entry-level positions. However, even applicants without a high school diploma are allowed to sit for a basic aptitude test. The primary criteria for hiring are the person's work ethic and trainability, rather than the level of education already attained. This gives people from poorer backgrounds with less opportunity to continue education an equal chance to compete for jobs. Applicants who pass the aptitude test are offered an entry-level job on the production line, where virtually every new entrant starts. The company has a strong policy of promotion from within, and all employees are eligible to compete for promotion. The system of continuing training prepares people to take more responsibility further into their careers at Yazaki-Torres.

Preference in hiring is given to women, unemployed and zero-experience applicants, differently able applicants, and janitorial workers interested in applying for entry-level positions on the production line. All these workers are paid on the basis of the jobs they occupy and given opportunities to develop their capacities and move into more responsible positions.

This approach to recruiting has had the beneficial effect of strengthening loyalty to the enterprise, making it easier for the company to retain good workers. In fact, Yazaki-Torres believes so much in the benefits of its policy of equal opportunity and non-discrimination that it is currently working on areas for further improvement.

Yazaki-Torres was aware of the subtle discrimination inherent in insisting on a minimum level of education. It chose instead to insist on a minimum level of aptitude, regardless of level of education attained, and to reach out to groups of workers who are often discouraged from applying for manufacturing jobs. Yazaki-Torres was able to make its recruitment philosophy a key component of its successful business strategy. Focusing on aptitude and trainability ensured that all recruits possessed the requisite level of attention to quality and detail that forms the basis of the company's marketing strategy. And providing employment opportunities for all in the localities where it operates has effectively cemented community relations, cut recruiting and retention costs, and nearly eliminated costs due to vandalism.

The following case shows how a company turned its policy of actively recruiting workers with disabilities into a successful business strategy.

Case 2. Walgreens: Tapping into the pool of workers with disabilities

Walgreens, an American retailer, has managed to expand its pool of applicants recently despite a tight labour market. Like many mass-market retailers, Walgreens operates on a small profit margin, which depends not only on sales, but also on highly efficient management of competent and motivated staff. Walgreens executive James M. Schultz and Professor Michael H. Le Roy explain:

> Even small changes in expenses related to sales and administration can turn a store's profit to a loss. At Walgreens, the most visible component of these expenses is payroll. Several years before passage of the Americans with Disabilities Act, Walgreens was confronted with a labour shortage. Operations people asked for special help to find employees. Human resources saw people with disabilities as a logical solution to this problem. Research showed that people with disabilities experienced higher unemployment, but nevertheless made good employees when given the opportunity. (...)
>
> For Walgreens, hiring, placing, and training disabled people began purely as a business strategy. Human resource practitioners recognized that most Walgreen managers reflected society's general ignorance about people with disabilities. A programme was developed to

show managers that their drugstores could operate well when staffed with people with disabilities. Instead of communicating this view in abstract terms to managers, research was undertaken to find stores that already made productive use of people with disabilities. This resulted in a training video to counteract existing prejudices and to begin the attitudinal shift that Walgreens needed for business reasons. (Le Roy and Schultz, in Ferris et al., 1995; see also Collins, 2001.)

The key to Walgreens' success was realizing that employing people with disabilities is primarily a question of attitude. Negative attitudes are deeply rooted and persistent. Walgreens directed its efforts to cultivating a more tolerant workplace, where people with disabilities would feel comfortable and be able to contribute fully.

Another example of a successful policy strategy is found in South Africa. This country faces a problem of HIV/AIDS, which, given its scope, is not only social, but also economic. The case below describes a company that viewed non-discriminatory recruitment policy as a part of corporate business strategy.

Case 3. Eskom non-discriminatory recruitment policy: People with HIV/AIDS[7]

Eskom is South Africa's state-owned national electricity utility. The company generates, transmits and distributes electrical power. It supplies 95 per cent of South Africa's consumption, which is more than half of all the electricity supplied on the African continent. Eskom is the fourth biggest utility in the world in terms of its installed capacity, and fifth biggest in terms of sales. Net profits for the Eskom Group in 2000 were US$227 million. The firm has approximately 33,000 employees working from more than 250 sites around the country. Most of its employees are male (86 per cent), most are aged between 30 and 49 (68 per cent), and most work in the lower job bands (60 per cent). And some of them live with HIV/AIDS.

Eskom launched its first formal HIV/AIDS policy in 1988, around the time that the first Eskom employee was diagnosed with full-blown AIDS. Throughout Africa HIV/AIDS was becoming a major health concern and Eskom management recognized the need to put formal policies and programmes in place. The company policy covered education, counselling, monitoring workplace incidence of HIV/AIDS, and protection against discrimination. However, the policy also included a controversial clause that required pre-employment testing and excluded HIV-positive applicants from employment. When management proposed to undertake a staff surveillance study in 1988, the unions rejected the proposal because they felt that Eskom's HIV/AIDS policy was

[7] Source: ILO, 2001c.

discriminatory in that it created barriers to employment. While Eskom's initial HIV/AIDS campaign was reported to have reached 98 per cent of the workforce by 1989, the programme seemed to be neither comprehensive nor coordinated.

Eskom began to move towards a more strategic and informed response to HIV/AIDS in the early 1990s. Senior management began to consider the long-term impact of HIV/AIDS on the workforce and the future viability of the business. Eskom's Chief Medical Officer engaged in debate with his counterparts in other organizations about discrimination and pre-employment testing. Furthermore Eskom's senior management soon realized that pre-employment testing was proving to be "self-defeating, not cost-effective and irrational" with a three-year expenditure of 200,000 rand (about US$17,785) detecting only 14 positive results from over 10,000 tests. Eskom's experience with pre-employment testing had demonstrated the futility and high cost of using this method to stop HIV/AIDS from entering the workplace.

When pre-employment testing was abandoned in 1993, the trade unions began to support the HIV/AIDS cause within Eskom. A policy review led to the development of a non-discriminatory HIV/AIDS policy, which includes education, self-awareness programmes, information sharing programmes, and care and support for the infected employees. As a result, according to the 2001 Eskom study, current prevalence of HIV among the employees is lower than the projected rate of 11 per cent. Moreover, a study commissioned by Eskom from the Harvard Institute for International Development found that the HIV/AIDS policy had a positive impact on the company's productivity.

The next case highlights the value of a comprehensive people-oriented management philosophy which is integrated into the firm's recruitment and selection policy.

Case 4. L&T: An integrated approach to recruitment and retention[8]

In 1991, India embarked on major liberalization and globalization of the economy, and opened its doors to a large wave of foreign direct investments and imports. Larsen & Toubro (L&T), an Indian conglomerate, decided to reinforce its leadership position in the new era of competition. The company set out to become a leading, world-class multinational, through commitment to total customer satisfaction, enhancing shareholder value, attaining global

---

[8] Source: Rajasekar and Gupta, 2001.

benchmarks and meeting the expectations of employees, stakeholders and society.

L&T has more than 8,000 employees. Attracting and retaining talent is a major challenge in a business oriented towards contract engineering projects, where on an average day almost 100 employees at all levels move to a new project location. In order to reach its goal, the company completely transformed its human resources strategy.

According to S. Chandrasekar, L&T's plant and human resources general manager, it is not only pay that attracts and retains good workers. Accordingly, the company has developed a range of complementary programmes to attract the best people and draw the best work out of them. These include:

- emphasizing a highly democratic management structure where workers are encouraged to express their opinions;
- devolving responsibility to front-line staff and encouraging initiative;
- equipping workers to assume more responsibility by establishing a world-class skills and leadership development system for all employees;
- encouraging workers to develop a plan of action to put training to better use;
- linking skills and leadership development to compensation;
- implementing a comprehensive accident prevention and safety programme; and
- developing an innovative employee welfare initiative, which includes welfare services and free health care for workers and the community at large.

In terms of sales, profits, assets and market capitalization, L&T ranks among the top ten companies in India's private sector. The company has gained prominence in intangible assets such as intellectual capital and brand worth; its technology base is considered to be on a par with the best in the industry worldwide, and most of its factories have secured quality certifications of the highest class. Company management believes that L&T success is largely explained by its attitude towards employees, who are treated with dignity and respect.

The various components of a comprehensive strategy for attracting and retaining workers will be examined in more detail in the following chapters.

ILS pertaining to recruitment

International labour standards emphasize the importance of non-discrimination in recruitment and selection.[9] Excluding people from consideration because of factors which have nothing to do with the job prevents firms from reaching the best workers in the community. And it further reduces the applicant pool, as many good candidates prefer not to work for a firm that discriminates in hiring.[10]

The Discrimination (Employment and Occupation) Convention, 1958 (No. 111), establishes that managers should not base their hiring decisions on any of the following criteria: race, colour, sex, religion, political opinion, national extraction or social origin.

The inherent requirements of the job should not automatically disqualify a particular category of worker, but should be tested on an individual basis. For instance, if a job requires heavy lifting, the manager should test applicants for their ability to meet this requirement rather than simply ruling out all female applicants. However, ILS recognize that it is reasonable to make certain distinctions between categories of applicants, such as the requirement that security staff be female in a women's prison.

It is important to guard against seemingly neutral hiring policies that have the unintended consequence of excluding some groups from applying. For instance, a strict dress code, which might prohibit any head covering, will discourage women from certain religious groups from applying although they may be highly suitable for the job.

ILS principles do not prohibit managers from taking proactive measures to hire members of groups that generally suffer discrimination; on the contrary, ILS encourage them to do so, as appropriate. As we saw in the Walgreens case, proactive measures send a strong signal to the target communities that the firm is serious about hiring the best workers the communities have to offer. These signals may encourage more people from disadvantaged groups to apply.

Certain ILS specifically address workers with disabilities. The most important of these is the Vocational Rehabilitation and Employment (Disabled Persons) Convention, 1983 (No. 159). This instrument encourages firms to develop a policy of hiring people with disabilities, which is consistent with its general business strategy. Managers should eliminate discrimination in the firm against persons with disabilities when no legitimate reason exists. Legitimate reasons relate only to the person's ability to perform the job or the firm's inability to bear the extra costs entailed in hiring a person with special workplace needs. Managers should provide information and training to staff

---

[9] Non-discrimination in conditions of work and promotion, which is equally important, is covered in Chapter 3.

[10] In addition to harming recruiting, discriminatory hiring practices may affect demand. Consumers are increasingly reluctant to purchase goods and services from firms with a bad reputation for discrimination in hiring. And MNEs increasingly scrutinize suppliers' hiring practices for signs of discrimination which could tarnish their brand name.

on integrating people with disabilities in the workplace, as Walgreens did with a training video. Lastly, enterprises should work with the government to develop ways of sharing any additional costs of hiring workers with disabilities, possibly through tax credits or other subsidies, bulk purchasing of special equipment, or training.

The case of Walgreens shows that promoting diversity in the workplace, through non-discrimination as well as through proactive recruitment and selection policies, can bring a number of important benefits. Managers can expand their pool of talent in the labour market. Good workers are commonly attracted to firms with a commitment to diversity. Employees are often proud to work in a diverse environment. This "feel-good" factor can boost general morale at the workplace. And policies and practices which encourage workplace diversity are good for public relations.

Excellent recruitment procedures are a key component of a successful business strategy. However, they are only the beginning of the story. Competitive firms must be able to keep good workers. The cost of turnover can be quite high. According to a study conducted at Merck and Co., a pharmaceutical company, the cost can run as high as 1.5 to 2.5 times the employee's annual income (Baron and Kreps, 1999). Even for jobs requiring less specialized knowledge, turnover costs can be extremely high (Schlesinger and Heskett, 1991):

In 1989, 119,000 sales jobs turned over in the retail network of the Merchandise Group of Sears, Roebuck and Co. With an estimated cost of $900 to replace and train a new sales associate, the annual turnover cost amounted to more than $110 million, representing 17% of the Merchandising Group's income that year. Even more importantly, Sears' own customer surveys revealed a strong negative relationship between store turnover and customer satisfaction.

NON-DISCRIMINATION 3

In Chapter 2 we discussed the strategic importance of not discriminating in recruitment. This chapter extends the argument by addressing diversity management – the importance of not discriminating in other aspects of management, such as compensation, job assignments, retention and promotion.

Treating workers fairly is a universal human value. In the workplace, this means basing employment-related decisions on various aspects of merit associated with performance on the job or demonstrated potential. Employees are not treated fairly when decisions are based on criteria that are unrelated to performance, such as race, religion, gender, or national origin.

At the beginning of the twenty-first century, two sets of forces are shaping and changing familiar organizational structures. First, organizations are finding that to succeed in an increasingly competitive environment, the traditional models for running business and governmental organizations no longer suffice and they must become more responsive to rapidly changing environments. They are thus relying more and more on finding new methods to improve efficiency and take advantage of available resources. The pressure leads organizations to adopt flexible approaches to the allocation and utilization of human resources, enabling them to distribute staff more efficiently, perhaps in inter-departmental, organizational and national teams, for better results. This is particularly relevant now, when globalization of markets and production requires people from different backgrounds to work together.

At the same time, changing workforce demographics are forcing organizations to review and revise long-held beliefs and policies concerning the people who work in these organizations. New organizational teams combined with changing workforce demographics are bringing more and more people from diverse backgrounds (in terms of gender, race, ethnicity, religion, national origin, age, disabilities – including HIV/AIDS – and many other characteristics) into contact with one another. Although national legislation and peer pressure have recently made a lot of enterprises treat their workers equally, the attraction, retention and advancement of a diverse workforce still require dramatic changes in corporate culture and management practice.

Unjustified difference in treatment or discrimination in its many manifestations, especially in employment and occupation, is still a major problem worldwide. The expression "discrimination in employment and occupation", refers to practices that have the effect of placing certain individuals in a position of subordination or disadvantage in the labour market or the workplace because of their gender, age, race, colour, religion, political opinion, national extraction, social origin or any other attribute which bears no relation to the job to be performed.

Discriminatory practices can be direct or indirect. Direct discrimination arises when an explicit distinction, preference or exclusion is made on one or more grounds. For example, a job advertisement for "men only" would constitute direct discrimination. Conversely, indirect discrimination refers to situations, measures or practices that are apparently neutral but which in fact have a negative impact on persons from a certain group. The latter type of discrimination, because of its more hidden nature, is the most difficult to tackle. The Deloitte and Touche case, presented later in this chapter, shows how indirect discrimination can be detected and addressed.

The principle of non-discrimination entails the equal treatment of individuals, regardless of any attributes other than their ability to do the job. Equality of opportunity and treatment allows all individuals to fully develop their talents and skills according to their aspirations and preferences, and to enjoy equal access to employment as well as equal working conditions.

To achieve full freedom from discrimination in employment and occupation, the mere removal of discriminatory practices does not suffice. It is also necessary to promote equality of opportunity and treatment in the workplace at all stages of the employment relationship, including recruitment, retention, promotion and termination practices, remuneration, access to vocational training and skills development. Diversity programmes, by recognizing and valuing the different backgrounds of employees and seeking to attract and retain the best qualified workers from all cultures and segments of the population, increasingly place equal opportunities at the heart of the human resources management approach. Moreover, non-discriminatory practices of diversity management are increasingly recognized as a managerial tool to increase efficiency and productivity.

The goal of managing a diverse workforce is to create a culture in which each employee has the opportunity to make a full contribution to the organization and to advance on the basis of excellent performance, which in turn contributes to the overall organizational performance and environment.

Although more women, older people and workers from minority groups are being hired, this is not enough to ensure successful diverse workforce management. Whether these workers remain in the organization and contribute to its success depends on how well the organization is treating them, on their opportunities for promotion, training, and career satisfaction. Companies invest in their employees with a view to developing their skills, loyalty and a long-term mutually rewarding relationship.

Although it is generally accepted that there is a positive link between equality at the workplace and good business performance, it is still difficult to draw enough evidence of the positive impact of non-discriminatory employment practices on corporate performance.

In fact, this is a priority topic for the ILO research agenda. For instance, the ILO (2000) has stressed that "further research should be conducted into intervening variables that determine the link between (...) equity and economic performance". The initial results of an exploratory study carried out by Perotin and Robinson during 2000 into the effect of non-discriminatory employment practices on productivity and performance support the propositions that:

- equal opportunity practices improve productivity;
- equal opportunity practices have a greater positive impact on productivity in those enterprises where discriminated groups form a higher proportion of the workforce;
- more active equal opportunity policies have a greater positive effect on productivity.

The findings of this study suggest that effective anti-discrimination policies may affect organizational performance in a number of ways (Perotin and Robinson, 2000, p. 560):

- labour is more efficiently allocated, increasing the quality of human capital and motivation, which improves organizational efficiency;
- there is a better match between individuals and jobs, more objective and systematic criteria for selection;
- members of the discriminated groups are more highly motivated due to better career prospects, an increased sense of fairness, and more rewarding assignments and opportunities for creativity;
- staff turnover is lower (particularly among discriminated groups);
- a less stressful work environment leads to better health, morale and dignity.

There is evidence of a higher impact on productivity when equal employment opportunity (EEO) practices are complemented by employee participation.

This chapter presents some examples showing how enterprises can introduce non-discriminatory management policies and practices which bring tangible economic benefits to the company. We start with an enterprise that has incorporated a large-scale diversity management programme with a number of interesting initiatives. This case shows how the company is trying to ensure that it treats all its workers equally well, even though it may not be treating them all the same. Many policies, such as those on working time and benefits, which appear to be non-discriminatory when uniformly applied, may, in fact, lead to differential outcomes because they do not take into account the particular needs of each worker.

Case 1. Miles, Inc., Pharmaceutical Division[11]

Miles, Inc., a North American Fortune 100 research-based firm with business in chemicals, health care, and imaging technology, is an independent operating company owned by Bayer AG, the German pharmaceutical and chemical giant. The pharmaceutical division has 6,000 employees and sales of US$1.4 billion in the United States and Canada.

As an American government contractor, Miles, Inc. has to comply with government regulations prohibiting discrimination on the basis of sex, race, colour, religion, or national origin. However, corporate leadership decided to go beyond mere compliance with the executive orders, and to make diversity an integral part of Miles' culture.

Sessa, Jackson and Rapini report as follows (Sessa et al., in Ferris et al., 1995):

> Both the corporation and the pharmaceutical division responded to the corporate-wide diversity vision by immediately implementing several initiatives designed to demonstrate that they were taking diversity seriously. The first initiative to be targeted was in benefits. The division created a family friendly benefits concept that incorporated both corporate programs already in existence (e.g., adoption benefits, personal and family leaves, wellness programs, employee assistance programs, and flexible benefits) with new benefits (e.g., job sharing, alternate work schedules, child-care referral services, on-site degree programs, and spousal relocation assistance). This first initiative was relatively easy to implement because it was an extension of previously existing programs that management already supported.
>
> As another immediate initiative, managers are held responsible for diversity management on their performance reviews and in bonus calculations. At the same time, the organization

[11] Source: Ferris et al., 1995.

began to advertise its seriousness toward the diversity effort through communications to employees and to the community.

At the same time that these initiatives were being put into place, the division fostered the development of a variety of employee input vehicles to help manage diversity on a longer-term basis on several levels of the organization. (...) Several groups including the sales diversity advisory group, the two research professionals task forces, and the gay and lesbian support group discuss issues and report to line managers of particular areas and sites. (...) Using these employee involvement groups as a model, management decided to develop a central group for the division to coordinate the specific site employee groups. This Division Diversity Group is composed of geographically and functionally diverse managers and it discusses diversity issues on a division-wide basis. The mission of this group is to recommend and review action plans for improving the pharmaceutical division's performance in hiring, promoting, and retaining employees from an increasingly diverse work force, with specific emphasis on women and minorities. The first three recommendations made by the group and adopted by management were: (1) a sexual harassment prevention education program for all employees; (2) a training program for all managers and supervisors designed to teach them how to manage people of diverse backgrounds, and (3) a managing diversity questionnaire to serve as a baseline and feedback tool to management regarding diversity issues in the workplace.

This diversity programme helped the pharmaceutical division of Miles, Inc. to start the process of cultural change and to set objectives and priorities that would allow the enterprise to stay competitive in the rapidly changing business and social environment.

The Miles, Inc. case describes an overall diversity programme undertaken by an enterprise. The next case looks at corporate non-discriminatory policy, aimed at better treatment of ageing workers. As in the case of Walgreens, presented in Chapter 2, skills shortage was the major economic rationale behind the policy. However, the issue here is not limited to recruitment, but to retaining a disadvantaged group of workers.

Case 2. The Grey Revolution at B&Q[12]

B&Q is the leading British Do-It-Yourself (DIY) and garden-centre retailer, selling about 45,000 different products. In the early 1990s the company began to expand internationally, first entering Poland and then moving into the Asian market in 1996. In August 2001, the biggest B&Q store in the world opened in Shanghai, China (17,000 square metres, almost twice the size of an average store in the United Kingdom).

B&Q's efforts to promote diversity in its workforce are strongly rooted in commercial realities. The link between diversity and business benefits is at the heart of B&Q's approach with "the emphasis of [its] diversity strategy (...)

[12] ILO, 2001d.

customer driven, developing policy from minimum compliance to best practice". A shortage of skills and the need to keep experienced workers were the main economic drivers behind B&Q's so-called "Grey Revolution", launched in 1989.

B&Q believes that workplace ageism is rife in the United Kingdom. The Institute for Employment Studies (IES) has found that between 25 and 34 per cent of employers in the United Kingdom impose explicit age limits on jobs (ibid.). The Government has estimated that at least 40 per cent of employers discriminate on the grounds of age (Ottaway, 1995). Whereas other European countries, including France and Spain, have age-related legislation (such as a ban on stating age limits in job advertisements), the United Kingdom has no legislation to prevent age discrimination.

B&Q and various non-governmental organizations (NGOs) argue that discriminatory employment practices related to age disregard significant social and demographic changes such as the rapid growth in the ageing population. More than 40 per cent of the workforce in the United Kingdom is currently over 45 years old. Furthermore, the past 15 years have seen a substantial decrease in the number of 20–24 year olds in employment.

In order to address changing demographics and the need for well-motivated retail staff with practical DIY home improvement and gardening experience, B&Q launched its "Grey Revolution" with a number of measures aimed at attracting and retaining older employees, including the introduction of the new over-50s stores.

B&Q's Lorian Coutts explains that the initiative was a reaction to severe shortages in the labour market at the time: "The adoption of our over-50s policy was, for the most part, a reaction to the changing job market in the late eighties. They provided an under-used pool of labour."

In addition, older people were thought more likely to have knowledge and experience in the DIY trade. The belief that older people would therefore provide better customer service was a key argument. This was supported by the results of subsequent B&Q customer surveys.

When Warwick University evaluated a new over-50s store against other stores, it found that the over-50s store topped the list in most measures. In her 1993 review of the Grey Revolution initiative, Mandy Jetter notes the following achievements: "a massive reduction in unattributable stock loss, a very low absentee rate, [and] the best sales award for the whole of B&Q." Other figures are cited by B&Q to demonstrate the success of the over-50s stores compared to other B&Q retail outlets:

- profits 18 per cent higher

- staff turnover 6 times lower
- absenteeism 39 per cent lower
- shirking 59 per cent lower
- improved customer perception of service
- increased skill base in the staff team

The next case shows how a firm identified discriminatory practices and tackled them.

Case 3. Deloitte and Touche: The Initiative for the Retention and Advancement of Women[13]

Deloitte and Touche, a worldwide accounting firm, did not think it was discriminating against its female workers – recruitment procedures were not gender-biased and female recruits were not dramatically outnumbered by males. However, female professionals were leaving the firm just as they reached the stage when they would be expected to bring in new clients and generate income. As senior management explained, in professional service firms the "product" is talent, billed to the client by the hour; managers were alarmed by the fact that so much of the firm's product was leaving. This problem led to an open dialogue within the firm that eventually resulted in serious changes in organizational culture and values.

Deloitte's *Initiative for the Retention and Advancement of Women* grew out of a 1992 task force chaired by Mike Cook, then CEO. Douglas M. McCracken, CEO of Deloitte Consulting, a global business of Deloitte Touche Tohmatsu, and also chairman of Deloitte & Touche LLP in the United States, explains:

> Nine years ago, we came to grips with the fact that women at Deloitte were on the march – out the door. In 1991, only four of our 50 candidates for partner were women, even though Deloitte & Touche – America's third largest accounting, tax, and consulting firm at the time – had been heavily recruiting women from colleges and business schools since 1980. Not only that. We also found that women were leaving the firm at a significantly greater rate than men.
>
> To be frank, many of the firm's senior partners, including myself, didn't actually see the exodus of women as a problem, or at least, it wasn't our problem. We assumed that women were leaving to have children and stay home. If there was a problem at all, it was society's or the women's, not Deloitte's. In fact, most senior partners firmly believed we were doing everything possible to retain women. We prided ourselves on our open, collegial, performance-based work environment. (…) How wrong we were, and how far we've come. (…) It took a cultural revolution, but Deloitte now has a radically different approach to retaining talented women. [The] results speak for themselves.

[13] Source: McCracken, 2000.

Today 14% of our partners and directors are women. While we aren't yet where we want to be, this percentage is up from 5% in 1991 and the highest in the Big Five. The number of women managing partners has increased dramatically, and we've eliminated the gender gap in our turnover: women now stay on at about the same rate as men each year. The firm's annual turnover rate as a whole fell from around 25% in the early 1990s to 18% in 1999, despite an intensifying war for talent. Besides saving us $250 million in hiring and training costs, lower turnover has enabled Deloitte to grow faster than any other large professional services firm in the past several years.

How did Deloitte achieve this? The company learned six lessons along the way.

1. Make sure senior management is front and centre. The initiative was always driven by the managing partners: it never became just an "HR thing" foisted on the firm.
2. Let the world watch you. Deloitte appointed an external advisory council and told the press about the initiative. The firm wouldn't let this initiative become just another "programme of the year" that led nowhere.
3. Begin with dialogue as the platform for change. Deloitte required all its management professionals to attend intensive workshops to reveal and examine gender-based assumptions in mentoring and client assignment. Mr. McCracken admits that:

   I myself saw it as just one more thing to do, and I had always been skeptical of HR-type programs. I'm sure I wasn't the only partner calculating in my head the lost revenue represented by two days' worth of billable hours, multiplied by 5,000 – not to mention the $8 million cost of the workshops themselves. (...) I was dead wrong. The workshops were a turning point, a pivotal event in the life of the firm. Through discussions, videos, and case studies, we began to take a hard look at how gender attitudes affected the environment at Deloitte. It wasn't enough to hear the problems in the abstract; we had to see them face-to-face.

   For example, an astounding finding related to career development within the firm was summed up by one of Deloitte's female partners: "Women get evaluated on their performance; men get evaluated on their potential."
4. Put the new attitudes to work with a flexible system of accountability. The findings from the workshops were translated into specific operational steps. The CEO and the taskforce set out clear expectations: "more of Deloitte's qualified women should be promoted, and the turnover rate for women should fall. But the firm had to be careful not to set quotas or seem to give women all the plum assignments. The key was to send a clear, powerful message for change while still giving heads of local offices some discretion." In 1993 local offices were asked to conduct an annual review to determine if the top-rated women were receiving their proportionate share

of the best assignments. The review confirmed the suspicions: women tended to be assigned to projects in non-profit, health care, and retail – segments that generally lacked large global accounts – while men received most of the assignments in manufacturing, financial services, and highly visible areas like mergers and acquisitions. After that, most offices began tracking the activities of their high-performing women on a quarterly basis in order to assure that the assignments were more equitable. Deloitte also started formal career planning for women partners and senior managers. This planning was so helpful that women suggested men be included, thus giving rise to Deloitte Consulting's current Partner Development Program.

A flexible system of accountability builds commitment. According to Mr. McCracken:

> Only after the operational changes had percolated through the organization did the task force introduce clear accountability for the changes that were being made. It offered offices a menu of goals derived from the Women's Initiative – such as a recruiting hit rate or a reduction in the gender gap in turnover – yet left it up to the offices to pick the goals best suited for their particular situations. Office heads started including their choices among the objectives that drove their year-end evaluations and compensation.

5. It's not just about women. It is necessary to promote a work–life balance for both men and women. Says Mr. McCracken:

> Moving toward equality in career development was fundamental. But as people began to discuss gender issues in workshops, meetings, and hallways, what started out as a program for women soon began to affect our overall corporate culture. (...) We discovered that work–life balance was important to everyone. [For example,] on paper, we had always allowed temporary, flexible work arrangements, but people believed – rightly at the time – that working fewer hours could doom an otherwise promising career. In 1993, only a few hundred people were taking advantage of the policy. So now we said that opting for flexible work wouldn't hinder advancement in the firm, though it might stretch out the time required for promotion. Use of these arrangements became one more benchmark of an office's progress with the initiative. And when a woman was admitted to the partnership in 1995 while on a flexible work arrangement, people really began to get the message. By 1999 more than 30 people on flexible work arrangements had made partner, and in that year the total number of people on flexible schedules had doubled to 800.

6. Make an airtight business case for cultural change. Mr. McCracken shows that the initiative had some positive tangible "bottom-line" implications for the firm:

> The task force prepared the firm for change by laying a foundation of data, including personal stories. Deloitte was doing a great job of hiring high-performing women; in fact, women often earned higher performance ratings than men in their first years with the firm. Yet the percentage of women decreased with each step up the career ladder, in all practices and regions, and many women left the firm just when they were expected to receive promotions. Interviews with current and former women profession-

als explained why. Most weren't leaving to raise families; they had weighted their options in Deloitte's male-dominated culture and found them wanting. (...) And all of them together represented a major lost opportunity for the firm. (...) As Cook (then CEO of Deloitte and Touche) summarized [in 1993]: Half of our hires are now women, and almost all of them have left before becoming partner candidates. We know that in order to get enough partners to grow the business, we're going to have to go deeper and deeper into the pool of new hires. Are you willing to have more and more of your partners taken from lower and lower in the talent pool? And let the high-performing women go elsewhere in the marketplace?

ILS concerning non-discrimination in the workplace

A number of international labour standards provide guidelines for managers seeking to ensure that their workers are all treated fairly. The most relevant instruments are the Discrimination (Employment and Occupation) Convention, 1958 (No. 111); the Equal Remuneration Convention, 1951 (No. 100); the Workers with Family Responsibilities Convention, 1981 (No. 156) and the Older Workers Recommendation, 1980 (No. 162).

Convention No. 111 stresses that a manager should not base decisions concerning job assignments, promotion or transfer on any of the following criteria: race, colour, sex, religion, political opinion, nationality, social origin, or marital or family status. Managers are also urged not to discriminate against other categories of workers, such as workers who are HIV positive. Managers who have taken the time to read this book are not likely to discriminate consciously against any of their employees. However, as the Deloitte and Touche senior management found to their surprise, a lot of discrimination is at a subconscious level, such as promoting women according to performance and men according to potential. Active measures should include policies such as flexible work arrangements or care leave to accommodate the varying needs of groups stemming from religious duties or family responsibilities.

Furthermore, managers should ensure that apparently neutral criteria do not inadvertently disadvantage certain workers in terms of assignments and promotions. For instance, workers should be assessed on the quality and quantity of output. Relying on other criteria, such as time spent at the workplace, may have an adverse impact on workers with family responsibilities, who may find it difficult to put in as much time as their colleagues.

ILS stress that managers, in cooperation with workers' organizations, should take active measures to eliminate *de facto* discrimination at every level. Examples of such measures include:

- educating all workers about the importance of eliminating discrimination in the workplace and raising awareness of subtle forms of discrimination that may not be consciously intended but still adversely affect some workers;

- carefully examining pay scales to ensure that differentials between categories of workers relate to differences in skills and responsibilities, not to the predominance of male or female workers; and
- paying special attention to the non-pecuniary benefits provided to employees, such as dependants' allowance, access to clubs and use of company equipment, which are often overlooked in enterprise policies on equal remuneration.

A thorough vetting of discriminatory policies in the workplace can be an enormous task, and some of the groups that benefit from discriminatory practices may resist change. But managers could have much to gain. A clear policy of non-discrimination underscores a meritocratic approach to hiring, compensation and promotion, which spotlights hard work and creativity as the keys to career advancement. These factors improve a firm's competitive position. Good workers will seek out firms where they know they will be rewarded for their hard work and will be more likely to stay. Firms which offer flexibility to accommodate employees' needs, rather than treating them as a homogeneous group, are more likely to be rewarded with flexibility on the part of staff in accommodating the needs of the enterprise. A good system to combat discrimination ensures that a company is not vulnerable to accusations of prejudice, which can severely damage its reputation among customers. Most importantly, a strong commitment to avoid discrimination between employees is essential to establishing an environment of trust and cooperation for effective social management.

WORKING CONDITIONS 4

4.1. Occupational safety and health

Treating workers with dignity and respect implies that concern for a safe and healthy work environment should be high on the employer's agenda. Cutting corners is not only a crime against people who suffer occupational illness or injury, but also bad for business. Table 1 shows that work-injury costs can be very high for society and for individual enterprises.

In 1993, on-the-job injuries and deaths cost the United States more than US$111 billion and 75 million working days. Table 1 shows how the tab breaks down.

Table 1. Work-injury costs

Costs	Billions of US dollars
Wage and productivity losses	59.9
Medical costs	20.7
Administrative expenses	14.4
Employer costs	9.7
Damage to motor vehicles	4.1
Fire losses	3.1

Source: "Accident Facts", National Safety Council, Itasca, IL, 1994.

The cases presented in this chapter show what companies can do to create a safe workplace: they also show that this policy pays off.

Our first case describes a company that introduced policies and practices aimed at reducing the number of injuries. These measures improved the safety of workers and also led to substantial savings due to a reduced workers' compensation insurance premium.

Case 1. Creation Windows, Inc.: A proactive approach to safe work[14]

In 1989, Creation Windows, Inc., an Indiana manufacturer of doors and windows for mobile homes, was averaging 200 workplace injuries a year in a workforce of 400 people. In other words, each year every second person was injured. After tracking how and where injuries happened, the company found that repetitive motion injuries were the most prevalent. Worse still, every injured person the company sent to a physician ultimately went into surgery.

At Creation Windows the production lines require workers to twist their hands and wrists a great deal, with many pinching motions. The consultants hired by the company found that even though some reaches were awkward, employees didn't realize they were hurting themselves.

The company took a proactive approach. A long-term safety and health education programme was launched. The firm supplied workers with gloves and wrist supports, and stopped using certain production techniques. It also replaced its man-sized tools with smaller ones for female workers. Further changes included job rotation, worker-management safety committees, and an awards programme.

Creation Windows also established a reporting system that catches most injuries early. For those who are injured, there is a new emphasis on conservative treatment, with surgery an option only where improvement is insufficient. And personal contact between HR representatives and injured workers helps to educate employees about their treatment and ensure that appointments are kept.

With this new programme, injuries plummeted. In 1994, the number of work-related repetitive motion injuries was less than 20 per cent of the 1988 figure. Creation Windows also got out of the assigned risk pool for workers' compensation insurance. The programme has boosted morale among employees and brought the turnover rate down.

Our next case provides an example of how occupational health and safety can be treated as part of an overall environmental awareness programme.

[14] Source: Sheley, 1995.

Case 2. Dow Chemical: Investing in the future[15]

In 1986, Dow launched its *Waste Reduction Always Pays* (WRAP) programme, whose charter is to generate economic benefit through waste reduction. Between 1986 and 1996 the WRAP programme yielded numerous cost-effective projects. For example:

- Process changes at an oxide derivatives plant in Midland, Michigan, resulted in an 88 per cent reduction in wastes to the incinerator, a 98 per cent improvement in yield, and annual savings of more than US$600,000 in raw material and incineration costs.
- Installing seal pots and double mechanical seals on feed pumps to the thermal oxidizer in a solvents plant in Plaquemine, Louisiana, eliminated a seal purge on the pumps as well as the need to incinerate perchlorethylene. This project led to waste reduction that saved Dow US$384,000 a year.

Based on this success, Dow decided in 1996 to set several important ten-year goals aimed at improving its environmental, health and safety performance worldwide. These goals will require a investment of about US$1 billion over ten years but should yield a 30–40 per cent return on investment by 2005 and more specifically result in the following projected savings:

- US$580 million in reducing energy use
- US$1.3 billion in reducing waste
- US$96 million in reducing process safety incidents
- US$50 million in reducing injury and illness rates
- US$34 million in avoiding costs incurred by business interruption, property damage or spill clean-up
- US$14 million in cutting by half the motor vehicle incident rate.

The total of these savings drawn from environmental improvements and protection of employee health and safety amounts to almost US$1.8 billion, or 1 per cent of the company's total revenues over ten years.

In 1996 a team of environmental, health and safety (EH&S) managers identified areas where environmental improvement was needed and others that offered high potential for economic benefit. Only those projects that met both criteria – yielding environmental and economic gain – were selected.

The costs and potential benefits of further improving performance were calculated. Historical capital spending and the costs of managing waste, cleaning up spills, and paying workers' compensation claims were examined.

---

[15] Source: World Business Council for Sustainable Development (WBCSD), 2000.

Preventing EH&S incidents increases plant reliability, minimizes risk exposure and maximizes asset utilization, all of which contribute to share value. Fewer spills and injuries mean less downtime, higher productivity and greater yield. Past experience shows that safety, quality and productivity in manufacturing are inextricably linked. These improvements can reduce Dow's costs by about US$200 million by 2005. For example, reducing the injury and sickness rate by 90 per cent will save about US$50 million by 2005. This money would otherwise be spent on meeting health claims and workers' compensation costs and on lost productivity due to absence. Additional cost savings will be achieved by halving the number of accidents involving Dow vehicles. If this goal is reached, about US$14 million will be saved by 2005 by reducing the cost of health claims, as well as vehicle repair and business interruption.

Progress on performance targets and cost reduction is routinely reported to the public. Finding economic benefit in EH&S progress is consistent with the principles of sustainable development. Dow has discovered that it can meet society's desire for sound and safe manufacturing, and its employees', shareholders' and other stakeholders' interest in a healthy, competitive enterprise.

The AIDS pandemic has forced employers to think more broadly about the health of their workers. The following case describes how employers in South Africa have responded to the HIV/AIDS crisis.[16]

Case 3. Health of South African workers: How companies respond to the HIV/AIDS challenge

By 2001, upward of 4.7 million South Africans were infected with HIV/AIDS (UNAIDS, 2000, cited in Segel and Sprague, 2001), and the number of HIV infected people is constantly growing. According to *The Economist*, "A typical South African company can expect a fifth of its workforce to die of AIDS in the next decade" (*The Economist*, 10 Feb. 2001). There is growing recognition that the costs of AIDS to companies will be significant. After much initial resistance, businesses have begun to estimate the costs to their organization, and to calculate the benefits of action to prevent the syndrome and to maintain the health of employees. The economic repercussions of HIV/AIDS in business were measured as reduced productivity, increased labour costs, loss of customers, and a further depression of profits from costs incurred through absenteeism, replacement, recruitment, training, increased payouts to medical schemes and employee benefits.

---

[16] We have already looked at a South African company that eliminated mandatory pre-employment HIV testing. In this chapter we discuss the HIV/AIDS problem primarily from the workers' health point of view.

The impact of AIDS on profitability is unpredictable, but probably huge. By 2015, South Africa's population is expected to be 23 per cent smaller than it would have been without AIDS, and per capita income will be no higher than today. This will affect demand for everything that South African firms sell. By one estimate (ibid.), each HIV infected employee costs a South African firm roughly twice that worker's annual salary. Additional indirect costs include the negative impact of AIDS on staff morale and accompanying disruption in the workplace; management and labour meetings to discuss AIDS as the crisis deepens, and loss of profit as the disease begins to affect the client base of the organization (Metropolitan Life, AIDS Research Unit, cited in Segel and Sprague, 2001). AIDS also hurts uninfected workers financially, as medical and other benefit resources dry up (*The Economist*, 10 Feb. 2001).

Most South African employers believe that the government has not responded adequately to the AIDS crisis, and that business therefore has to play a larger role in halting the disease in the workplace. Dr. Clive Evian, a community health specialist and Director of AIDS Management and Support at Metropolitan Life, one of the largest insurance companies in South Africa, emphasizes that the workplace plays a vital role in containing the disease in South Africa: "Employees are 'captives', attending the same place day after day, it [the workplace] has the most available financial and people resources, and it has a vested interest in preventing as much of the problem as possible" (Metropolitan Life, AIDS Research Unit, 2001, cited in Segel and Sprague, 2001). Dr. Jack van Niftrik confirms: "The bald answer lies in private sector initiative. Much as some employers may dislike the fact, they must accept that their long-term survival lies entirely in maintaining a reasonably productive workforce" (van Niftrik, 2000, in Segel and Sprague, 2001). The threat of losing employees is exacerbated by the fact that South Africa's economy is characterized by an acute shortage of skills. Companies may have to replace sick employees with workers who are less experienced or less skilled.[17]

So, HIV/AIDS is a "bottom line" problem for many South African enterprises. What have they done to tackle it?

Many South African companies invest a lot of time and money in studying the specific impact that HIV/AIDS might have on the well-being of their workers and enterprise bottom-line performance. Efforts are also aimed at studying ways to prevent the spread of disease.

Many South African enterprises are setting up AIDS prevention programmes, which range from distributing free condoms to educational theatre,

[17] The argument follows the same logic as that of Deloitte and Touche.

to voluntary testing and counselling. For instance, AngloGold, the largest South African gold-mining company, hands out AIDS leaflets in various African languages to miners and their girlfriends, and hires specialists to train "peer educators", miners who teach other miners about safe sex, as well as prostitutes who teach other prostitutes. AngloGold also offers voluntary HIV testing and counselling. And South African Breweries (SAB) conducts role-playing exercises to show how quickly infection can spread.

At regional level, Coca-Cola Africa, the largest private employer in Africa, has adopted minimum standards on ensuring that people with HIV/AIDS do not suffer discrimination in the workplace. The standards require local producers and distributors to form AIDS committees which include representatives of management, human resources, labour organizations and medical personnel. Coca-Cola Africa is deploying its unique infrastructure and presence to support AIDS education, prevention, and treatment programmes in local communities. For example, in Zambia, it is providing assistance to the Family Health Trust, an education project that works with young people in more than 2,500 anti-AIDS clubs throughout the country. And in Nigeria, Coca-Cola is supporting the work of the National HIV Sero-Prevalence Sentinal Surveillance Survey for women attending antenatal clinics, and providing marketing support to advertise the project.

In some cases, a company's medical services may be the only source of health care in a community. Compagnie Fruitière, a major banana producer which operates in Cameroon, Côte d'Ivoire, and Mauritania, has committed to providing medical care, vaccinations, prevention programmes, laboratory and pharmacy services, and maternity clinics. Such a substantial commitment to the well-being of the community sends a strong signal that Compagnie Fruitière is a place that cares about its workers. Consequently, the company has no difficulty in recruiting and retaining reliable workers.

Mondi, a paper-making MNE, also goes beyond preventive measures. Mondi provides health insurance, drugs and nutrition supplements to infected workers, as well as job rotation to lighten tasks. And all Mondi staff are trained to perform several different jobs so that they can cover for their sick colleagues who need to stay at home to rest.

ILS concerning safe work

Many international labour standards deal with health and safety issues, the most comprehensive instrument being the Occupational Safety and Health

Convention (No. 155), adopted in 1981. The occupational health and safety standards are intended to protect workers from physical danger in the workplace and to reduce the social cost of an unsafe workplace to the worker, the firm and society. The ILS contain several key principles.

Management should develop and implement a policy and programmes to ensure a safe working environment. Dow's success rested largely on its comprehensive approach, rather than relying on piecemeal actions. The policy and programmes should be developed in cooperation with workers' representatives. This is extremely important because workers generally have a better sense of the potential hazards and more ideas for ways to improve safety and health. Their cooperation and support is also needed to ensure that preventative measures, such as wearing safety equipment, are actually followed. Furthermore, employee involvement encourages workers to share responsibility for occupational health and safety. Creative Windows' success in improving its injury rate is largely due to the joint committee it formed on workplace safety and health.

Managers should provide adequate safety equipment and organize sufficient training and motivation to ensure that protective equipment is worn and that safety rules are followed. In addition, managers should post important information and instructions in conspicuous places. Managers should also cooperate with labour inspectors, not only because the law requires this, but because inspectors may have useful information to share.

Management should periodically review and update company health and safety policies in light of advances in research. Some ILS have schedules of maximum exposure levels, which are updated periodically in line with the most recent scientific findings. Lastly, managers should respect the right of employees to refuse to return to work if they have legitimate fears for their health or safety.

These ILS guidelines can contribute generally to better management practices and to recruitment and retention. Providing a safe and healthy work environment enables a company to attract better-qualified workers and to keep them; it also reduces turnover and increases organizational commitment. A dangerous workplace sends the message that a firm is uncaring, which can damage relations with the immediate community and generate bad publicity for the firm.

ILS principles on safe work can also affect a firm's competitive edge more directly. A safe workplace reduces employer contributions to workers' compensation funds, which are generally experience rated: it may also reduce wage bills in tight labour markets where employers would otherwise have to compensate workers for accepting more dangerous jobs.

4.2. Working time

Working time is one of the critical conditions of work, having a direct impact on the day-to-day life of workers and on enterprise performance (Clerc, 1985).

> The level of hours of work and the way those hours are organized can significantly affect not only the quality of working life but also the quality of life in general. They can influence the health of the worker, safety at work, the degree of strain and fatigue, the level of earnings, the amount of free time available, the extent to which that free time represents usable leisure, the family and social life of the worker – in short, many of the elements that determine a worker's well-being.

At the same time, working time is an extremely important issue for an enterprise. "Hours of work can be a factor – in some circumstances, a major factor – determining output, cost of production and ultimately the profitability or viability of the [enterprise]" (ibid.). Ways of organizing working time can have an immediate effect on product quality and they can affect absenteeism and turnover.

Overtime is one of the most common issues. Some overtime is essential to give enterprises the flexibility to deal with fluctuations in demand, unexpected problems or other special circumstances. However, frequent and substantial use of overtime can lead to negative consequences for both workers and the enterprise. From the workers' side, it can have a negative effect on health, safety and well-being. From the enterprise point of view, it can result in lower product quality and higher costs, caused by shirking during the regular hours. The following case shows how enterprises can successfully address overtime reduction.

Case 1. Reduction of overtime in the Asian footwear industry

A study of 14 factories in three countries (China, Thailand and Viet Nam) supplying sports shoes to three leading global MNEs supports the idea that reducing overtime does not necessarily have a negative impact on enterprise performance (Bodwell and Rogovsky, forthcoming).

In the mid-1990s the main footwear MNEs adopted Codes of Conduct and they required their suppliers to comply with them. Working time was very high on the list of changes demanded of suppliers and, at the same time, it was one of the most difficult for factory managers to comply with. Changing from a system where a factory would work whatever hours were needed to get the job done (in the peak season up to 80, even 100 hours a week) to one where it was limited to 60 hours per week (including overtime) has required the supply factories, as well as the MNEs themselves, to change in various ways.

Accounting and information systems were needed to keep track of hours worked, and bonus systems were put in place to encourage higher productivity to make up for lost output. Most importantly, training was provided to explain to workers and managers why the change was necessary. Given the seasonal nature of the sector, with its peaks of demand, change has not been easy. As a labour practices inspector of one of the MNEs put it:

> Overtime is the biggest challenge to meeting the Code, due to the nature of the business. In the low season, we can't lay off the workers, and then we don't have enough for the high season. We can't use temporary workers, because they don't have the skills – these take several months to learn.

Over time, the factories have learned to boost productivity and to meet the same production goals within the working-time limitations. Many of the supplier managers were surprised to find that this was possible – by setting limits and paying bonuses, they were able to meet their goals.

One of the suppliers has achieved good results through complying with an MNE Code of Conduct, particularly the provisions on hours of work. This factory has only about two years' experience with the MNE Code of Conduct. At first, there was quite strong resistance and doubt about the benefits of the Code for the factory and the workers. Now factory managers attribute tangible results to the changes in working time (ibid.). Turnover in this factory fell from 4 per cent in 1998 to 2 per cent in 2000. At the same time, orders from the MNE rose by 10 per cent between 1998 and 2000. The CEO of the multinational actually visited the factory and expressed his satisfaction with the efforts to comply with the Code. Now over 3,000 job applicants are on a waiting list for positions. Working hours have fallen, but productivity has risen quite considerably. In 1998 workers put in about 300 hours a month. When the Code was introduced, the factory had to bring the workweek down to the code standards – a maximum of 250 hours a month, including overtime. Output fell in the beginning but was back at previous levels by the end of 2000 (about 400,000 pairs of shoes per month), resulting in a considerable net productivity gain during the period.

ILS pertaining to working time

Numerous international labour standards provide guidelines on working time.[18] These instruments aim to guarantee adequate periods of rest for workers. Managers should ensure that workers have sufficient rest between

[18] The main instruments include: the Forty-Hour Week Convention, 1935 (No. 47); the Weekly Rest (Industry) Convention, 1921 (No. 14); the Reduction of Hours of Work Recommendation, 1962 (No. 116); the Weekly Rest (Commerce and Offices) Convention, 1957 (No. 106); the Weekly Rest (Commerce and Offices) Recommendation, 1957 (No. 103); and the Holidays with Pay Convention, 1936 (No. 52), and Recommendation, 1936 (No. 47).

shifts. Maximum hours of work should average no more than 48 per week, and should progressively drop to 40 hours per week. Employees performing particularly strenuous or dangerous tasks should work fewer hours as appropriate.

Although seven days is the standard period of time over which to average hours of work, managers can also use longer periods (a month, for example) when their need for labour fluctuates more. Managers should ensure that a decent standard of living is maintained despite any reduction in working hours; otherwise, workers will be forced to accept extensive overtime, which defeats the purpose. Of course, managers should take into account the needs of the enterprise, but in a way that is consistent with the workers' need for periods of rest. Instead of requiring many hours of overtime from workers, for example, management should consider hiring more workers for an additional shift.

Each worker should be allowed a day of rest, comprising at least 24 consecutive hours. Managers should aim to extend weekly rest to up to 48 hours. Although managers must be allowed to require workers to temporarily forgo their day of rest, this exception should be reserved for genuine emergencies and not be a routine way of scheduling workers. Any day of rest which is worked should be compensated with another day off, and in no case should a worker go more than three weeks without a day of rest. The day of rest should generally coincide with the traditional day of rest in the community, and management should make efforts to accommodate various religions.

After one year of service with an enterprise, a worker should be entitled to paid annual leave. Any legitimate sick leave taken during the year should not jeopardize the right to holidays with pay. Annual leave is intended to ensure that workers are given a minimum period of leisure to recuperate and spend time with family, friends and community. Therefore, managers should be careful not to break it up into short periods which might not be adequate for travelling to see the family. Annual leave should be at least six working days, excluding any public or customary holidays. Workers should receive the salary they would be entitled to had they worked during that period. And workers with more years of service with the enterprise should be granted longer leave periods. On all aspects of working time, managers should consult with the union or workers' representatives. Rules relating to working time should be conspicuously posted in the language of the workers, and records of working time and annual leave should be kept.

Adequate rest ensures that workers are sufficiently fit and nourished to carry out their tasks effectively and that product quality is higher and more uniform. Healthier workers also reduce the risk of occupational accidents. Indeed, reasonable hours of work should be an integral part of any occupational health and safety policy. As we saw in cases such as SAS Institute and Deloitte and Touche, setting reasonable limits on working time can help a firm to attract and retain more qualified workers who value a balanced life. MNEs in a variety of industries, and their suppliers, are facing increased consumer pressure to ensure that working hours are not excessive.

HUMAN RESOURCE DEVELOPMENT 5

All over the world, skilled workers are in great demand. They can often choose among job offers and command higher wages. We have already discussed the implications that the ongoing "war for talent" might have on management policies and practices. However, we have not yet talked about another set of policies and practices that can help an enterprise improve the quality of its human capital – human resource development (HRD). This chapter presents case studies that show how HRD has enhanced productivity, and gives some examples of how HRD can be achieved in a variety of cost-effective ways.

We start with an example of how global competition has motivated an entire industry to invest substantially in HRD, and the important role the unions played in maximizing firms' return on their investment.

Case 1. HRD strategy in the Mexican clothing industry[19]

The clothing industry in Mexico is labour intensive. Approximately 80 per cent of workers are classified as non-skilled, and there is a shortage of skilled labour in the industry. The vast majority of workers are female. Investment in new technologies is relatively low.

The industry was badly hit during the 1980s with the opening of trade and structural adjustment, which decreased internal demand. Apparel manufacturers generally switched from producing goods to providing assembly services for clothing to be exported. As a consequence, the Chamber of Industry began by pushing for more labour market flexibility (working hours and types of contract). However, with intense competition and limited ability to change the legal restrictions on hours of work and types of contract, the Chamber began

[19] Source: Garcia, Romero and von Bullow, 1996.

to rethink its strategy. Employers found it difficult to recruit motivated or qualified workers with experience, because clothing is a low-prestige industry. The changes in the government's HRD policies and programmes around this time encouraged the Chamber to use training as a means of coping with economic and market changes and of attracting good workers to the industry.

Training accelerated during the 1980s and 1990s and changed in content, to better meet the needs of employers and workers. Employers state that this contributed to a market for training agencies and to a training culture. Recently, 97 per cent of new recruits have received training in the apparel industry. Employers are mainly motivated by the desire to develop skills so that workers can rotate between jobs within the same wage level, increasing flexibility. They also hope that increased production will allow higher wages, which can be increased to attract new recruits. Training typically comprises not only manual skills but also attitudes, familiarity with productivity, quality, modern production techniques, and productivity workshops for managers.

Although government-funded training centres existed for the industry, employers were reluctant to hire graduates because they lacked practical experience which employers valued very highly. A critical evaluation of training in the clothing industry, commissioned by the employers' association, found that the system needed to promote more substantial involvement of trade unions and workers in training efforts. The stumbling block was a general lack of harmonious labour relations. Firms did not appreciate the potential of training to strengthen labour relations (defined as more worker involvement in company objectives). Only 1.3 per cent of firms reported that one of their objectives in providing training was to improve labour relations, which is quite low compared with similar industries such as fabricated textile products, where 16.3 per cent of firms report that motivation. Consequently, the average productivity gain from training in the apparel industry was 32 per cent, while the gain in fabricated textile products firms averaged 40.3 per cent. The report concluded that aligning the interests of workers and firms is important for maximizing potential productivity increases from training.

The next case, also from Mexico, shows the importance of not only providing training, but also of motivating workers to use that training to best effect.

Case 2. General Motors in Mexico[20]

The car industry in Mexico is relatively high tech and capital intensive, with

[20] Source: Garcia et al., 1996.

a high percentage of foreign direct investment. It exports approximately 43 per cent of production. Firms are of all sizes, from micro-enterprises to large companies. Many producers are subsidiaries of foreign firms.

The car industry took off in Mexico in the late 1970s. Influenced by the increasingly popular Japanese model of car production, the industry adopted a strategy that focused on training and a high degree of worker involvement to improve quality, productivity and ultimately competitiveness. As of 1991, workers were receiving formal training in the following proportions: 96.1 per cent of large firms, 77.5 per cent of medium-sized firms, 64 per cent of small firms and 17.5 per cent of micro firms.

GM-Mexico invested particularly heavily, with substantial payoffs. According to a plant manager at a subsidiary of GM:

> The plant was picked in 1991 as the best in North America. For the company, this success is directly linked to training: people have made us reach levels that many plants have not been able to, plants with more technology in place. The reason is the emphasis that our management gives to education, training, people's development (...) doing things well the first time; continuous improvement. The three basic goals [are] making world-class products, having world-class people and making world-class productivity commitment. An employee is trained when he comes on the job and throughout his stay with the company. When they first come on the job, we have an introductory programme that [includes] some basic topics we call "mandatory", topics that will always be useful for them, and that they all have to take; for example, performance evaluations synchronized manufacturing.

Another GM manager explains the training process:

> Once in a plant, the employee goes through about two and a half months (it can be as long as six or even seven months) of training in the company's training centre. This training is divided into three stages: first, basic training, in which they are exposed to all the very specific organizational concepts [we work with], [second], instruction tailored for a specific work area; and [third], technical and maintenance training. The training centre has a simulated production line where the workers can train on different operations. Part of the course is carried out in a classroom and part on the [production] floor. Both technical and attitudinal training are emphasized, teamwork, motivation, placing people in the most appropriate job. Safety is [also] stressed.
>
> The company has attempted to optimize resources for training and so is setting up a single training system; with the workers from outsourcing plants, it will include about 70,000 employees. [It will be] the training network for GM in Mexico. That way we are going to lower costs and eliminate duplication; we will be able to have advisory services for all organizational planning of all training processes [as well as] exchanges with US and European GM.

Once trained, workers are motivated to use their new skills by rotating their job assignments and providing opportunities for career advancement. They also link improvements in the quality and quantity of work to pay.

"Training policy is stipulated in the collective bargaining agreement and in an additional agreement which establishes very clearly the benefits accruing to the worker who completes training and evaluation programmes."

GM-Mexico closely evaluates the outcome of training, particularly as it relates to improvements in the quality of output and productivity.

Another way to motivate workers is through issuing certificates. For workers, training is valuable if it enhances their job mobility, either within the firm or between firms. Certificates which verify that a worker has successfully completed a training module enhance mobility and are a good means of motivating people to participate. In the Mexican automobile industry as a whole, 54 per cent of companies issue training certificates to employees who successfully complete various modules. Firms, in cooperation with the government, are committed to making the certification process formal and transferable, to help jobseekers and employers in both internal and external labour markets.

Case 3. La Fragua, S.A.

La Fragua, S.A., a Guatemala-based retailer operating in Guatemala, El Salvador, and Honduras, has developed an effective strategy to motivate workers to use their training. All employees receive introductory and continuing training, regardless of position held. Training programmes have been developed to orient workers, increase their productivity, and prepare them to assume new responsibilities. Workers are motivated to use their training to the fullest through annual profit sharing schemes. In addition to providing employees with vacation allowances and education grants, each store belonging to the company distributes 10 per cent of after-tax profits to its workers in the form of vouchers to be used to purchase merchandise or repay loans. This policy has contributed substantially to La Fragua's success in expanding its market share in Latin America.

Training is only one part of an effective HRD strategy. Employers can also improve workers' skills through work organization efforts related to enriching jobs. This approach allows workers to use a whole variety of skills and gives them more responsibility and experience in decision-making. The next few cases show a range of possible activities aimed at human resource development through work organization. We start by looking at work organization changes at the level of job description, to see how a job that most people would consider boring and not creative can become interesting.

Case 4. Job enrichment of a teller position in a bank-holding company

A major American bank-holding company decided to enrich the job of bank teller. Tellers were given more responsibility, authority, and accountability so that they would feel more professional and satisfied in their jobs. A total of 526 tellers participated in a study carried out at intervals of 6, 24, and 48 months (Griffin, 1991, cited in DuBrin, 1997). The results of the study indicate that job enrichment substantially motivated the tellers and helped them improve their skills. Although performance did not increase initially, it improved significantly when measured at 24 and 48 months.

This case shows how employees' individual performance and skills can be improved without promoting people or moving them from one job to another. The next case, however, looks at job rotation as a way of upgrading workers' skills and productivity.

Case 5. SATS Security Services: Improving workers' skills through job rotation[21]

SATS Security Services (SSS), established in 1965, is a wholly owned subsidiary of Singapore Airport Terminal Services (SATS), which is itself a subsidiary of Singapore Airlines. It encompasses an auxiliary police force which provides security services to airlines and other related organizations at airports in Singapore. The majority of its staff members are police officers trained to use a wide range of sophisticated security equipment.

SSS is in the forefront of aviation security, covering aircraft and passengers. Its services include baggage identification, boarding pass and passport check, cabin search, security for VIPs, guarding aircraft, passenger profile screening, travel document forgery detection, X-ray and other screening of baggage, sniffer screening and onboard air marshals, guarding and escorting inadmissible passengers, access control, CCTV monitoring, investigations, crime prevention advice, training and consultancy. The company grew from a staff of 450 in 1989 to 760 in 1999.

Job rotation, combined with a team approach, is an essential element of SSS. Normally, a worker moves to a new section after two years, and no one is allowed to stay in a particular job for more than five years. From the officers' point of view, the system provides variety and increasing responsibility. For the firm, job rotation ensures that officers do not become too

[21] Source: ILO, 2001e.

familiar with other employees or those they are guarding, which might make them complacent or open to corruption. It also ensures that all employees acquire knowledge of the whole company and its various functions.

Better qualified staff make a substantial contribution to SSS performance. One of the most important measures of company performance is the clients' rating of service quality, as revealed through the annual survey of clients. This has shown a continuous improvement throughout the decades, at least partly related to the move toward job rotation. Enterprise success is also reflected in other measures such as crime detection rates and baggage and cargo pilferage reports. For example, in 1993–94 there were over 70 reports of cargo pilferage for just under 0.5 million tons of cargo handled, while in 1998–99 there were 20 reports for a total cargo of 1.2 million tons. There were almost 200 reports of baggage pilferage in 1994–95 for a total of 25 million tons of baggage handled, while in 1998–99, although there were still about 200 reports, the total volume of baggage handled had risen to 33 million tons.

The next case, also from Singapore, shows how job rotation and multi-skilling could become part of a long-term career development programme linked to innovative changes in organizational structure.

Case 6. Sheraton in Singapore[22]

The hospitality industry has been very hierarchical in its organization, with command and control systems and top-down communication, but little horizontal communication. The management structure typically consisted of multiple layers of authority, frequently as many as twenty-five.

People with few skills and a low level of educational achievement were typically recruited. Low salaries were prevalent, but the industry did offer career prospects within a specific function such as catering, with progression from waiter to general manager. Jobs were tightly demarcated, from bellboy to waiter to receptionist. An employee's experience was frequently limited to a single functional area and might not include all the jobs within that area. Those who progressed did not necessarily have business acumen. People who stayed in the industry had to accept the long hours demanded by a 24-hours-a-day, 365-days-a-year industry. Human resource practices were often rudimentary; for example, decisions about promotion and recruitment were often made on the basis of subjective judgements and assumptions.

Senior management started to question whether this structure was capable of delivering improvements in productivity, efficiency and customer satisfac-

[22] Source: ILO, 2001f.

tion. Changes were radical. They amounted to a reengineering of the industry and the introduction of many high performance work practices. The hotel management hierarchy was reduced from 25 to ten levels. Managers took a fresh look at the distribution of jobs. Rather than organizing work tasks in terms of function, they were restructured in bands consisting of jobs that required the same set of skills. This produced ten levels from the entry jobs at level 1, to the general manager at level 10. Levels 8, 9 and 10 were the decision-making grades; levels 5, 6 and 7 were the trainee managers and department heads. Levels 1, 2, 3 and 4 were the operational levels, with waiters at level 2 and supervisors at level 4. Level 1 entry jobs were bellboys and room attendants.

Once the bands were established, the next task was to focus on multi-skilling within each band. Employees were expected to master all the skills at their level. Training and job progression were then determined by the need for all the staff to become proficient in all the jobs within their band. This involved moving staff through all the jobs in their existing band. Once they were multiskilled within their band, having become proficient in three or four different jobs, they would be ready for promotion to the next band. There the process would start again, and the person would learn all the tasks within that band before moving up to the next level. The result was that department heads were skilled in all functions from finance to HRD and that staff were not only more flexible but also more highly skilled, in the sense that they had a much broader understanding of hotel operations.

The approach to continuous improvement was inspired by the Deming tradition. The basic idea of process mapping was applied within the broad bands. Using external consultants, the traditional pyramid was effectively inverted, putting the operational staff at the top, driving the process, because these people were in direct contact with the hotel clients.

Job creation and multiskilling delivered a number of advantages. It made the jobs more demanding and satisfying for the employees. It trained future managers in the full range of functions and ensured a practical knowledge of all aspects of running a hotel, including the necessary business acumen. Those who moved up the hierarchy, "career spiralists", acquired a considerable depth of knowledge and very high levels of skill. Of course, not all employees are climbers, and the ideal position is that about 40 per cent are motivated to move between bands, with the remaining 60 per cent content to remain within their band.

The other advantage was that staff at each level could back each other up as needed. If there was a rush in the coffee shop and waiters were under pressure, then staff could be redeployed from another function to maintain a high level of customer service and satisfaction. They simply had to change their uniform. This would cost more at the level of coffee shop management, but for the organization as a whole it was a far more productive and efficient use of staff resources.

Such an approach has been adopted by several international hotel chains. Marriott (case 10 below) provides another example of a hotel chain pursuing good HRD policies and practices. By maintaining a people-orientation, these hotel chains reduce staff turnover and, as a result, achieve competitive advantage in an industry where turnover is running at more than 50 per cent for line-level employees (ILO, 2001g).

The next case looks at a global organization which believes its people are critical to corporate success. In order to improve the quality of its employees, it uses such HRD techniques as delegating responsibilities and rotating jobs, in the context of international operations. These practices allow the company to be extremely decentralized but still in control and, as a result, successful.

Case 7. AES: A decentralized company with global values

The AES Corporation is a radically decentralized power generation company operating more than 100 plants in 19 countries. All plants, from Argentina to Pakistan to Kazakhstan, are run by teams working in a highly decentralized fashion. With more than 10,000 employees, AES has a headquarters staff of less than 30 people, and no centralized staff functions. O'Reilly and Pfeffer (2000) explain:

> There is no strategic planning department; no specialized staff in human resources, quality assurance, or environmental compliance; no legal department to speak of; and the CEO sees his job primarily as helping and training other people to raise capital and perform the treasury functions. Business development is the responsibility of almost everyone in the firm, including relatively junior people, not just something done by senior executives or a business development group.

Very few people will doubt that AES is a successful company. In late 1999, its return on equity was 178 per cent of the industry average and its profit margin was 203 per cent of the industry average (Wall Street Research Net, 1999). The company has achieved a 5-year growth rate of 41 per cent in revenues and 18 per cent in earnings per share. The total return to shareholders over the previous 5 years was a stunning 531 per cent; not bad for an "old economy" company.

What has allowed such a decentralized company to maintain control of its global operations and be successful? AES follows a set of universally accepted, people-oriented values, which are clearly manifest in its human resource policies. These values differentiate AES from its competitors and help it to be successful.

Roger Sant, AES chairman and cofounder, elaborates:

I suppose our underlying assumption about people – especially AES people – is the most important. (…) The organization has assumed that their people are good, that they really want to make a difference; that you don't need to control them; that you can depend on them.

This belief is echoed in the AES Annual Report statement: "The people of AES are not principally economic resources. We are not tools of the corporation. Rather, we hope the corporation is structured to help individuals make a difference in the world that they could not otherwise make."

This people-oriented philosophy is translated into management practices. AES corporate leaders maintain that management practices must come from the company's core principles and values. Otherwise, "it's just technique" (Wetlaufer, 1999). AES hires people mostly for their aptitude and cultural fit, rather than their specific skills. It then rotates staff between various jobs with increasing responsibility and emphasizes learning new skills. Delegation of responsibility gives a feeling of meaningfulness and significance. Continuous job rotation at AES gives people the opportunity to learn and use a range of skills. Formal training and development are also emphasized. For example, AES has a tuition reimbursement programme that covers 80 per cent of costs for employees taking classes at local educational institutions.

The organizational culture of trust and respect is translated into a policy that allows people at AES to make honest mistakes. According to O'Reilly and Pfeffer (2000), that's what AES leaders believe in: if you put people in new jobs and give them lots of responsibility, they will make mistakes. Errors are part of any learning process – think of learning to ride a bicycle. AES encourages people to take on new responsibilities and try new things by not punishing honest mistakes. For instance, at the plant in Barry, Wales, when a technician forgot to submit a bid to the government pool on a day when demand was high and prices at a peak, he cost the company $150,000 in a single hour. The plant manager didn't fire him, and the technician later proved his worth by designing a daily, fail-safe alarm so the mistake would never happen again (O'Reilly and Pfeffer, op. cit.; AES Annual Report, 1997).

People at AES are put in charge. Therefore, they need to have full information at hand. Sharing information is an important part of the company's HRD policy. In fact, AES shares so much information with its employees that all of them are considered to be insiders by the Securities and Exchange Commission guidelines. For instance, O'Reilly and Pfeffer (2000) tell us that:

(…) at the Thames plant information on financial and operating performance is shared once a month at a communications meeting. During the meeting, each operations area of the plant talks about its projects, reports on personal news, and discusses anything that concerns people or is on their minds. Some people voluntarily come to these meetings even on their day off.

AES implements its human resource policy and general decentralized management style even in plants it acquires. There is often a transition period from the traditional, hierarchical system to the AES way. Sometimes this period is lengthy, but AES never compromises on its values. And it eventually succeeds, despite operating in 19 different countries. Why? Because it has tapped into some human values that are virtually universal. Who doesn't want to be treated with respect? Who doesn't want to be treated fairly? AES shows that respect, dignity and trust are something that appeal to everybody, all over the world. If a multinational has a set of universally sound values and principles and well-trained employees, it can decentralize decision-making, significantly delegate authority, and still profit substantially.

The next case looks at an enterprise that has made human resource development a key part of its market strategy, aimed at becoming a sole supplier for a subsidiary of a Japanese MNE.

Case 8. Delco-Remy

Japanese car manufacturers expanded their American production in the early 1980s. Delco-Remy, an American battery manufacturer, realized that in order to become an American supplier for a major Japanese MNE, it needed to adjust its business culture to fit better into the Japanese system of participative management. Delco-Remy therefore launched a large-scale training programme in participative management. This training paid off, since it allowed Delco-Remy to become a sole supplier of batteries for Honda of America. Delco's Keith W. Wander tells the story (Schuler and MacMillan, 1984):

Honda of America was seeking an American battery manufacturer as a supplier to its auto plant in Marysville, Ohio. Honda wanted a plan that had a participative system of management and a reputation for producing a quality product at a competitive price. After a contact from the Delco-Remy Sales Department, two American representatives from Honda visited the Delco-Remy plant in Fitzgerald, Georgia. This visit was followed by a second one with Mr. Hoshita, President of Honda, in the group.

During the second visit, plant tours were conducted by Operating Team (hourly employees) members. The tours were followed by Operating Team members explaining to Mr. Hoshita how people were involved in the Fitzgerald business, how Fitzgerald and Honda could be mutual resources to each other because of their participative systems, and why a Delco battery was the best-built battery in the world.

Mr. Hoshita returned several months later to ask more questions of the Support Team (salaried employees) and Operating Teams. Shortly afterward, Honda of America announced Delco-Remy, Fitzgerald, as a sole supplier of batteries, based upon its (1) culture; (2) quality; and (3) price, in that order.

It is common knowledge that a good HRD programme can help employers attract good workers. Even in industries where it is very difficult to recruit and retain employees, due to limited career potential, the prospect of training can motivate people to apply. Here is a particularly creative example that shows how companies can team up to create synergies in recruitment and retention (Cappelli, forthcoming).

Case 9. Cascade and Burger King: Training as a recruiting and retention device

Cascade Engineering, Inc., a plastic parts manufacturer, and the local Burger King operations have sought economies by pooling their recruiting and selection efforts. Applicants who do not have the skills for Cascade's production positions but who seem to be good workers are offered a job at Burger King in the first instance. And Burger King employees, who are otherwise expected to turn over quickly, are offered vocational counselling and the possibility of better positions at Cascade in the future as both a short-term retention device and an incentive to work for Burger King in the first place.

Pre-employment training programmes also can help a company attract and retain workers. In addition to reducing turnover costs, pre-employment training may be viewed as an investment in the community, which can create a number of additional benefits to the organization (Rogovsky, 2000). The next two cases show how training programmes can help companies improve the quality of their labour pool.

Case 10. Marriott International: Benefits of pre-employment training

Marriott International combines recruitment and training through some truly innovative management practices. This internationally recognized hotel chain introduced Pathways to Independence, a training and orientation programme aimed at welfare recipients. This segment of the labour market is important for hotels since a lot of jobs require very basic skills and do not pay well. Marriott's programme takes into consideration the background of participants and attaches great importance to being sensitive rather than judgmental. J.W. Marriott, Jr. and K.A. Brown stated: "For many, this is the first opportunity they'd had to master skills that most of us take for granted. (…) Trainers help trainees overcome self-esteem problems, family troubles, and other challenges" (Kanter, 1999). Professor Kanter from Harvard Business School explains: "Over two-thirds of the company's 131,000 employees are entry-level, lower-wage workers in housekeeping, engineering, security, maintenance, food service, and reservations. Developing an effective method to recruit, train, and retain workers in these positions has always been a critical concern." Throughout the 1980s, Marriott had reached out to untapped pockets of the labour market, such as Viet Nam veterans, ex-offenders, the disabled, recent immigrants, and welfare mothers. Although the company received tax credits as a financial incentive, Marriott continued to be plagued by a high level of turnover and poor job performance. By the beginning of the 1990s, the company badly needed new sources of reliable labour. After some experimentation, the first viable Pathways programme was launched in Atlanta, Georgia in 1991. Since then, Marriott has not only reduced turnover rates but also improved job prospects in inner cities.

Pathways to Independence is a very sensitive programme that hones the job skills, life skills, and work habits of welfare recipients, and the company guarantees participants a job offer when they complete the training. This programme has brought some tangible benefits to the company:

> About 70 per cent of Pathways's graduates are still employed by Marriott after a year, compared with only 45 per cent of the welfare hires who did not participate in Pathways and only 50 per cent of other new hires. And success in the Pathways to Independence program has encouraged Marriott to undertake other initiatives such as the Associate Resource Line, a hot line that provides assistance with housing, transportation, immigration, financial and legal issues, and even pet care. It cost Marriott $2 million to set up the hot line; it now saves $4 for every dollar spent, through lower turnover and reduced absenteeism.

Another example of pre-employment training is taken from the United Kingdom. Like Marriott International, Thorn Lighting invests heavily in pre-employment training. However, while Marriott trains mainly in sensitivity and customer service, Thorn, being a manufacturing company, pays more attention to such issues as teambuilding, health and safety, and assembly workplace competencies.

Case 11. Thorn Lighting[23]

Thorn Lighting, Ltd., based in the United Kingdom, is one of the world's leading suppliers and manufacturers of lighting systems and products. With operations in 30 countries, 11 of which have manufacturing facilities, Thorn

[23] Source: ILO, 2001h.

sells to customers in 140 countries. The group employs 4,200 people worldwide, including 1,800 in the United Kingdom across ten sites, three of which involve manufacturing operations.

Since 1989, Thorn Lighting has undergone major organizational and cultural changes enabling its market share to approximately double. In 1998, sales increased to GBP£392 million (US$561.5 million) and the operating profit was GBP£26.4 million (US$37.8 million). Much of this success has been attributed to more effective performance management and teamwork.

Since 1994, Thorn's Spennymoor plant in the United Kingdom has run a series of work experience courses in which local, unemployed people, including school leavers, visit the factory to observe working conditions and receive training. The courses are run in partnership with local bodies, as a service to the local community and as a recruitment device. The courses were designed to meet the company's need for a ready pool of flexible individuals who could fulfil the need for temporary, short-term labour in line with new working practices. Generally, people enter the company through the pre-employment training route on a temporary short-term contract. If they are still with the company after six to 12 months, they are normally confirmed as permanent employees.

The frequency and number of training workshops are dictated by the labour needs of the individual manufacturing teams. Workshops are run only if there are not enough trained people in the database who are ready to work at short notice. A strong working relationship has been forged with the local Employment Service. When extra staff are required, the Employment Service pre-screens candidates to discover how they would best fit into Thorn, rather than to sort them into selected and rejected candidates. The courses last from three and to ten days, and introduce trainees to Thorn and its processes. They cover basic business knowledge, teambuilding, health and safety, and assembly work. Trainees participate in a two way continuous assessment.

During the training, individuals still receive state benefits as they are technically available for work. The company does not pay the trainees but does provide free meals. Travel expenses are paid by the Employment Service, and trainees do not perform work with any commercial value.

On the last day of the course, trainees receive a Certificate of Achievement. This Certificate has become widely respected by other employers. The trainees are then placed in a database, and Thorn gives them preference when vacancies arise.

By the end of May 1999, a total of 329 people had completed the Spennymoor programme, and 150 of these had gone on to full-time employment with Thorn. A significant number of the remainder have found permanent employment elsewhere. Due to the success of these courses in placing people, Thorn has expanded the programme.

A number of benefits have accrued to the trainees, the company, and the community since the scheme began:

- The database provides a pool of potential employees already inducted and partly trained.
- The training period is, in effect, an extended interview, thus allowing Thorn to assess a person's character and potential.
- When employed, trainees are able to contribute fully much faster.
- Thorn is contributing more than its share to increasing the skills base of the local population.
- Thorn has received significant positive publicity, both locally and nationally.
- The programme has earned Thorn a reputation as the best place to work in the community.
- The strength of the partnership with the local Employment Service often means that Thorn has the pick of employees and trainees before other local companies.
- The programme has had a positive benefit on Thorn's own internal teambuilding.
- The programme is a partnership between management, the workforce and unions.
- Thorn successfully presents its community work as part of its overall image without appearing self-righteous or insincere.
- Trainees are often hired by other companies, which is good public relations for Thorn.
- The overall "feel good" factor creates an impact with subcontracted lorry drivers who are knowledgeable and clearly proud to be associated with Thorn.

In addition to reducing turnover costs, pre-employment training can be viewed as an investment in the community that can create a number of additional benefits to the organization (Rogovsky, 2000).

All the companies mentioned in this chapter invest heavily in human resource development. This may be surprising, as it is becoming more difficult to retain increasingly mobile workers. However, as Peter Cappelli explains:

> Some companies still make substantial investments in employee development. General Electric, for example, has the oldest management development program in the US, dating from 1919, providing two years of general management training and work experience to college graduates in areas like finance, human resources, information systems, and

engineering. Other companies known for developing managers like SmithKline, Pepsi, and Procter and Gamble can offer diverse work experience within the same corporate structure because of their broad holdings and also by giving real responsibility early on. At the same time, corporate recruiters love to poach from these companies in large part because of the management development they offer. So why do the companies continue to offer it? One important reason is that it helps them with their own recruiting, even if retention takes a hit down the road. Applicants know that going with a company like GE or Pepsi gives them a real opportunity for advancement at other companies – precisely because recruiters will be interested in hiring them away. (Cappelli, forthcoming.)

It is necessary to work out whether the value added that companies gain from training these employees is higher than the turnover costs multiplied by the probability that they will leave. However, as we saw in the case of SAS Institute, people-centred policies can substantially reduce this probability, making it rational to invest in people despite the general trend towards increased mobility. Furthermore, companies invest in people who may leave, at the same time as other enterprises are training people who may join. This situation encourages companies to work together with governments and employer organizations to develop the quality of the workforce in the labour market as a whole. The Mexican garment industry provided a positive example of this approach.

ILS pertaining to human resource development[24]

International labour standards addressing HRD issues aim to:

- promote investment in skills development at all levels;
- ensure the broadest possible access to education and training; and
- maximize the return on investment in HRD, including at company level.

ILS stress the importance of a solid basic education which focuses on literacy and numeracy. A literate and numerate workforce provides the foundation for firm competitiveness, and increases the return on investment in on-the-job training.

ILS draw attention to the need for continuous upgrading of workers' skills for an optimally-trained workforce. Continuous training can help a company improve its competitive edge, by increasing the productivity of existing workers and helping to attract better workers. Investing in workers' skills can also improve the firm's image and boost worker moral and loyalty.

Employers are encouraged to work with government and workers' organizations on skills certification programmes. The examples of the car and textile

[24] The Human Resources Development Convention, 1975 (No. 142), and Recommendation, 1975 (No. 150). The Recommendation is in the process of being updated to address current training issues such as IT skills.

industries, as well as Thorn Lighting, demonstrate the importance of certifying skills learned on the job and through formal training programmes. Certification gives workers more mobility in the job market and helps employers to verify a worker's skill level. Well-trained workers who can compete better in the labour market are less resistant to retrenchments. And independent certification of skills provides more reliable information on the abilities of job applicants.

The Mexican Chamber of Garment Industry realized the importance of including trade union issues in its HRD programme to promote positive industrial relations. Managers should involve worker representatives in developing and evaluating firm-level HRD policies and programmes. Lastly, managers should ensure that there is no discrimination in firm-level HRD policies and training as unequal access to training will result in unequal treatment in other areas such as job assignment and promotion.

The Human Resources Development Convention, 1975 (No. 142), also encourages employers to work with government to develop national HR policies and programmes at all levels, from basic education through continuing education. The return on investment in staff training depends crucially on literacy and numeracy skills. Employer input into the quality of the workforce in the whole national labour market increases the likelihood that workers will have essential basic skills, which increases the firm-level return on investment in training.

LABOUR RELATIONS: FREEDOM OF ASSOCIATION, COLLECTIVE BARGAINING AND EMPLOYEE PARTICIPATION IN DECISION-MAKING 6

A discussion of people-oriented values and approaches to management would not be complete without a look at the relationships between management and unions or other workers' representatives. There are several ways in which unions can help advance the effectiveness of the organization. First, they provide a credible mechanism for addressing the grievances of individual employees. Even the most enlightened managers find it difficult to maintain credibility in dealing with complaints from individual workers as they arise. Processes for dealing fairly with such complaints can help diffuse them and prevent them from affecting the rest of the organization. Second, unions provide a mechanism to identify concerns that need to be resolved through collective bargaining before they begin to have an adverse impact on performance. There are many issues, such as safety and health, where the goals and interests of unions and management are similar and where they can easily work together.[25]

The cases presented in this chapter demonstrate that labour–management partnership is an integral part of progressive management practice, and may even provide the foundation for introducing a new management style. The cases illustrate three major principles:

- the importance of freedom of association and protection of the right to organize;
- the value of collective bargaining and dispute settlement; and
- the contribution that employee participation, cooperation and communication can make at the enterprise level.

[25] For a detailed overview of the literature on unions' effect on enterprise performance, see Freeman and Medoff, 1984, and Pfeffer, 1998 (in particular, Chapter 8).

6.1. Freedom of association and collective bargaining

We start with some cases which show that recognizing the right of workers to organize and bargain collectively can help an enterprise to succeed due to a good industrial relations climate. First, let us consider the example of Southwest Airlines. This is a successful company, well-known for its egalitarian culture and participative management style. At the same time, it is the most unionized airline in the United States, and a lot of observers attribute its success to its healthy industrial relations climate.

Case 1. Southwest Airlines: How good labour relations can contribute to the bottom line[26]

Southwest Airlines is one of the most heavily publicized corporate success stories. It has grown in 30 years from a four-plane carrier into the fifth largest airline in the United States, as of 2000, worth US$4 billion and employing 29,000 workers. Table 2 provides some data on the company's performance.[27] Southwest consistently has the lowest costs and the best customer service as measured by on-time performance, lost bags, and customer complaints. Condé Nast Traveller has ranked Southwest as the safest of the world's 85 major airlines. It is the only American airline to have made a profit every year for the past 26 years. Employees work hard; they are committed and do not want to leave. Southwest's people-oriented values, attitudes and behaviours resulted in Southwest being rated as the top company in *Fortune* magazine's 1998 list of "The 100 Best Companies to Work for in America".

Although much attention has been drawn to Southwest's intense focus on operations, customer service, charismatic leadership, strong organizational culture, and innovative management practices, the basis of its success is its philosophy of treating its workers with respect and dignity. These values have enabled Southwest to establish and maintain high-quality labour–management relations.

Herb Kelleher, former CEO of Southwest, describes the company's approach:

> It used to be a business conundrum: Who comes first? The employees, customers, or shareholders? That's never been an issue to me. The employees come first. If they're happy, satisfied, dedicated, and energetic, they'll take real good care of the customers.

[26] Source: O'Reilly and Pfeffer, 2000.
[27] Source: Southwest annual reports.

Table 2. Southwest Airlines' financial summary

	1995	1996	1997	1998
Total operating revenues (millions of dollars)	2 873	3 406	3 817	**4 164**
Operating income (millions of dollars)	314	351	524	**684**
Return on average total assets (percentage)	6.0	5.9	8.0	**9.7**
Return on average stockholder equity (percentage)	13.7	13.5	17.4	**19.7**
Size of fleet	224	243	261	**280**

When the customers are happy, they come back. And that makes the shareholders happy (Godsey, 1996).

This philosophy is reflected in Southwest Airlines' mission statement: "We are committed to provide our employees a stable work environment with equal opportunities for learning and personal growth" *(http://www.iflyswa.com).*

Southwest puts this belief into action by treating all its employees with equal respect and dignity. It uses very few part-timers and does not contract out as much as many other airlines. The company has never had a layoff, which is very unusual in the airline industry. Employees exercise their right to participate in recruitment. Teamwork and multifunctional teams are emphasized. The company has a policy of full disclosure of financial and operational information to all employees. And Southwest values character over competency; it is one of the very few companies that have an official policy of no punishment for honest mistakes. Its official policy states: "No employee will ever be punished for using good judgement and good old common sense when trying to accommodate a customer – no matter what our other rules are" (*New York Times*, 14 Mar. 1999).

Southwest's compensation practices also aim to give its employees a feeling of belonging and ownership. Heavy use is made of collective, as contrasted with individual, rewards. For example, profit sharing and stock ownership are emphasized over individual pay for performance. Executive pay is relatively low for the industry and executives are expected to share in any wage freezes the same as any other employee. But what is truly surprising is that the level of pay at Southwest is at or below the industry average. At the same time, the number of job applicants per opening is one of the highest in the industry. Libby Sartain, Southwest Vice-President for People, a title that reflects the company's approach, explains: "We want people who are not looking for a job, but rather who are looking for a cause" (Hoffer, 2001).

Many people are willing to take a wage cut to join Southwest, and many have turned down more lucrative offers from competitors.

With such a strong people-oriented management style it may come as a surprise to know that Southwest is the most unionized airline in the United States – 84 per cent of its workforce is unionized. Far from being redundant, union representation makes people-oriented management possible. Unions are the most efficient vehicle for workers to convey their expectations, ideas and concerns to management. The airline industry is generally characterized by adversarial industrial relations; no doubt many readers have experienced at least one delayed flight due to a strike. Yet, in its 30-year history Southwest has had only one walkout (by the mechanics in 1980) because it takes the unions seriously and accepts that they are the voice of workers.

Southwest Airlines has long-term collective agreements. Recently the pilots' and dispatchers' unions ratified 10- and 12-year agreements respectively, which is very unusual for this industry, known for labour–management confrontation. Both agreements emphasized gains in stock rather than wage increases. Management believes in the notion of social dialogue. It helps union members and negotiators to research their pressing issues and to conduct employee surveys before each contract negotiation. Jim Parker, current CEO and Vice-Chair of the Board, believes that: "Most labour disputes are not really about money. There is something else at stake – respect" (ibid.). And Southwest culture is all about respect. Says Colleen Barrett, President and Chief Operations Officer: "We are very proud of our employee relations. We treat people with respect" (ibid.).

Treating people the way they deserve to be treated pays off. Southwest employees demonstrate much higher levels of productivity than employees of other airlines. For example, Southwest people routinely turn an aircraft round in 15 minutes from the time it arrives at the gate until it leaves.[28] Continental and United average 35 minutes for similar activities. Southwest gates are typically staffed by a single agent and a ground crew of six, rather than the three agents and 12 ground crew of other airlines. As another example of higher productivity, in 1998 Southwest had an average of 94 employees per aircraft whereas United and American had almost 160. The industry average was over 130. Southwest served more than 2,500 passengers per employee in 1998 while the industry average was about one thousand.

[28] Rapid turnaround of aircraft means that planes are in the air more, actually earning revenue.

Case 2. NUMMI: You only live twice[29]

New United Motor Manufacturing, Inc., (NUMMI) is an extremely successful automobile plant, known for its innovative high performance management systems. These systems co-exist peacefully with a union–management system of industrial relations. Moreover, a lot of experts believe that good labour relations at NUMMI are a factor that allowed the plant to establish innovative management systems and achieve success.

Year 1982

In 1963, General Motors opened an automobile assembly plant in Fremont, California. By 1978, this plant employed over 7,200 workers. By 1982, it was closed.

General Motors had a lot of sound reasons for closing the plant:

- GM-Fremont ranked at the bottom of GM's plants in productivity and was producing one of the worst-quality automobiles in the entire GM system;
- the union averaged 5,000 to 7,000 grievances per three-year labour contract;
- the plant was characterized by high use of sick leave, slowdowns, wildcat strikes, and sabotage;
- first-line managers were carrying weapons for personal protection;
- daily absenteeism was almost 20 percent;
- drug abuse and alcoholism plagued the workforce.

There was a climate of fear and mistrust between managers and workers. This is how George Nano, union representative at this GM plant, described labour relations there: "It was war. At GM we had to fight for everything. Management just did not seem to care. And when management doesn't care, workers won't care either" (O'Reilly and Pfeffer, 2000).

Year 2001

In 1983 General Motors signed a letter of intent with Toyota to re-open the plant, now called New United Motor Manufacturing, Inc. (NUMMI). Toyota wanted to gain a foothold in the American market, learn about working with American suppliers, and see if their manufacturing and management approaches could work with American employees. GM needed a small car (the Nova) to add to its product line and hoped to learn about Toyota's production

[29] Sources: O'Reilly and Pfeffer, 2000; Adler, 1993; Rogovsky, interviews at NUMMI, 1995–96.

system. Doug Fraser, then President of the United Auto Workers (UAW) union, saw this as an interesting opportunity and committed the union to work with the new venture. Don Ephlin, UAW head for GM also made a commitment (Adler, 1993).

Now NUMMI is one of the best plants in the industry. It employs over 4,000 union members and produces an average of 87 vehicles per employee, far above the 50 cars per worker at both Saturn and Buick City, the most efficient GM facilities (O'Reilly and Pfeffer, 2000). In 1998 NUMMI won the National Association of Manufacturers' award for excellence. The award noted that this plant managed a changeover to a new model in the remarkable time of only five days and took only 30 days to reach full production. The quality of the new vehicles, already one of the highest rated, was nearly 50 per cent better than the old version, while the cost-reduction targets through the launch were exceeded by 86 per cent. In addition the workforce made over 3.2 suggestions per person in 1998, of which 81 per cent were adopted. Over 86 per cent of the plant's team members made suggestions that year, leading to savings of over US$27 million (Productivity Consulting Group, 1999).

This is the same plant, the same union and, surprisingly enough, the same workers – NUMMI offered recall rights to the ex-GM plant workforce, 85 per cent of whom accepted. So, what made all the difference?

A tale of two plants

The explanation is simple – the difference in management systems and approaches. New management (mainly Toyota executives), introduced the Toyota system of lean manufacturing, which depends crucially on trust and respect for workers. This system emphasizes teamwork, job security, employee involvement, and worker self-confidence. The system makes all employees responsible for quality and safety and provides a method (the *andon* cord) for any person to stop the line to get help with a quality or safety problem. The estimated cost of line downtime is US$15,000 per minute, and the cord is routinely pulled over 100 times per day (O'Reilly and Pfeffer, 2000).

The new system also promotes an egalitarian culture and team approach. NUMMI has three levels of management, compared to five or six levels at other GM plants. All workers at NUMMI are part of a three–six member multifunctional team, run by a team leader, who is not a manager but a union member selected jointly by management and the union.

This new management system could not have been implemented successfully in a hostile union environment, which, unfortunately, is not such a rare thing in the automobile industry. NUMMI operates in an environment characterized by peaceful industrial relations based on labour–management dialogue.

O'Reilly and Pfeffer (2000) state:

From the beginning, the NUMMI system has relied on a unique relationship between the union and management. [The union] has supported the NUMMI production system, including the team concept, (...) job classifications, nonconfrontational problem solving (asking "why", not "who").

In return for this support, NUMMI management:

- recognized, right from the first day, the same union (UAW, Local 2244) that represented workers at GM-Fremont;
- agreed to pay union-scale wages;
- agreed to reappoint the union bargaining committee;
- asked union leaders under the old system to resume their role;
- agreed that team leaders (the key production position at NUMMI) should be selected jointly by union and management;
- agreed to a no-layoff policy;[30] and
- signed a new collective agreement.

The new collective agreement starts by stating:

Both parties are undertaking this new proposed relationship with the full intention of fostering an innovative labour relations structure, minimizing traditional adversarial roles and emphasizing mutual trust and good faith (NUMMI internal document, 1993, cited in O'Reilly and Pfeffer, 2000).

Union–management relations of trust and mutual respect are clearly evident when comparing the new and old contracts (see table 3).[31]

Interestingly, the old contract ran to over 1,400 pages in eight booklets, while the new one needed only one booklet of less than 100 pages. Why use paper when the trust is already established? As one of the NUMMI union leaders put it: "It's hard to say what's the role of the union, what's the role of the company. It doesn't work that way. It's a partnership. It's a total rethinking of your role" (Levander, 1990).

The examples of Southwest Airlines and NUMMI both show that managers' recognition of the principle of freedom of association and the right to organize can create a healthy industrial relations climate, which in turn helps the enterprise to be competitive.

Freedom of association is closely linked with the right to bargain collectively. The effect of collective bargaining on management development has

[30] This was a significant move – 80 per cent of employees feel that job security is the most important aspect of working at NUMMI.

[31] Source: O'Reilly and Pfeffer, 2000.

Table 3. NUMMI: Old and new contracts

Old GM contract	New NUMMI contract
UAW and GM "recognize their respective responsibilities under federal, state, and local laws relating to fair employment practices."	UAW and NUMMI "will exhibit mutual trust, understanding, and sincerity, and, to the fullest extent possible, will avoid confrontational tactics."
"Employees will be laid off and rehired in accordance with local seniority agreements, with management giving 24-hour notice."	"The company will take affirmative measures before laying off any employees, including such measures as the reduction of salaries of its officers and management."

been studied by many experts, most of whom reached the following conclusion long ago (Slichter, Healey and Livernash, 1960):

> Collective bargaining seems to have greatly encouraged the development of management. (...) Companies that have been relatively successful in union–management relations gave evidence of following wise basic policies, of negotiating balanced general policies, of developing good implementing and procedural arrangements to make policy effective at the operating level, and of having considerable initiative in labour relations administration. The challenge that unions presented to management has, if viewed broadly, created superior and better-balanced management, even though some exceptions must be recognized.

Management and unions can and should be partners. Their cooperation, based on mutual respect and trust, can create a true win-win situation. The following short case shows that even when the market situation apparently requires wage cuts and other measures not particularly favourable to the workers, labour–management cooperation can lead to mutual gains.

Case 3. Crown Zellerbach Corporation

Crown Zellerbach Corporation, an American manufacturer, and the International Woodworkers of America demonstrated that even in an industry downturn with widespread wage cuts, a competitive advantage can be gained without reducing total wages. The union and management agreed to an incentive pay plan by which workers were able to earn about US$3 more per hour than before in straight wages. Because this incentive system made the workers more productive, management also involved the union in a broad range of issues. Thus, the workers gained in involvement and salary and the company gained in cost reductions and greater competitiveness (Schuler and MacMillan, 1984).

Further examples illustrating the importance of social dialogue and collective bargaining come from the Caribbean region where recently an increasing number of enterprises have started to improve the quality of labour–management relations. These include state-owned and private enterprises, domestic enterprises and subsidiaries of MNEs, small and large enterprises, export oriented and domestic market oriented enterprises. The growing importance attached to good labour–management relations is, to a large extent, explained by changes in the mindsets of both employers and worker representatives. It has become clear that adversarial relationships are destructive for enterprises – they diminish productivity and profits, and more generally make for an unpleasant place to work.

The following examples are taken from three different countries and three different sectors of the economy. The case of Trinidad Cement Limited shows how international competition made a company and union re-think their approach to labour–management relations in an effort to turn the company round. The Alcan Jamaica Ltd. case describes how a tripartite agreement, reached at industry level and translated into an action plan, improved the competitive position of a company. Finally, the case of the St. Vincent Electricity Company (VINLEC) shows how collective bargaining can be a starting point and a driving force for large-scale company restructuring.

Case 4. Trinidad Cement Limited: A case of successful collective bargaining driven by international competition

Trinidad Cement Limited (TCL) is an international company that operates in Trinidad and Tobago and more recently in Barbados and Jamaica. Its experience illustrates how market pressure can make both management and unions rethink their relationship and join their efforts to make the company economically successful and a nice place to work.

Established in 1954, TCL has had poor labour–management relations for most of its existence. According to the CEO, Mr. Rollin Bertrand, managers believed in "ruling with an iron fist" and trade unionists were accustomed to an adversarial approach to labour–management relations (Bertrand, presentation at Caribbean Enterprise Forum, 2001). Between 1984 and 1995 TCL averaged two full or partial work stoppages a year with an estimated cost over the period of US$42 million in today's dollars; it also had 47 unresolved grievances/disputes, of which nine went to the Ministry of Labour and three to the Industrial Court. The collective bargaining process was often protracted, with the conclusion of negotiations taking as long as 12 years. Largely due to the dysfunctional relationship between management and unions, plant availability and efficiency were below 70 per cent.

In the mid-1980s TCL started to feel increased pressure from international competition (Thai Cement and other international companies). The company had to re-think its management style in order to remain viable. Finally in 1995 management realized what had to be done in order to improve corporate performance and create a good industrial relations climate. As in many other cases described in this book, changes had to start with a re-examination of the fundamental corporate philosophy and values. Management came to realize that workers and their representatives must be treated as strategic partners and stakeholders, since workers are the company's most valuable asset. TCL created an HR Vision Statement (box 1) that expressed management's belief in the importance of workers for corporate success.

Box 1. TCL: Vision Statement

To create a family of employees within the TCL Group of Companies where individuals feel confident that they are participating, contributing, recognized and rewarded for the success of the Company. The Company should be a place:

Where employees are valued as precious, special people, secure in the knowledge that the Company will at all times seek their long-term interests and be supportive in times of need

Where health and safety concerns are paramount and accidents are non-existent

Where the Company is concerned about employees' family life and creates work systems and after-work activities to support this ideal

Where employees really feel that the Company sees them as individuals, encouraging self-development, growth, progress and advancement, not only in their careers but also in their personal lives

Where honesty, integrity, fair play, trust and respect abound and employees feel pride in their association with the Company and each other

This statement was translated into an action programme, called "PEOPLEING", that included:

- tripartite committee/partnership forums;
- transformation workshops with a special focus on people;
- non-crisis forums;
- a revised performance management system;
- a new negotiation strategy; and
- departmental meetings and focus groups.

Table 4. Employee satisfaction survey results

Factors surveyed (summary)	1996 results (as a %)	1999 results (as a %)
Overall index	52.05	62.29
Job satisfaction	69.89	74.93
Stress (lower = less stress)	57	50.67
Annual performance evaluation	48.08	58.78
Advancement opportunities	42.86	48.67
Remuneration and benefits	56.24	62.88
Supervisor–employee relationships	56.36	68.45
Management–staff relations	57.61	66.36
Industrial relations climate	42.21	57.8
Communications	39.2	57.44
Physical conditions	57.72	69.49
Company values and image	68.33	79.23

Management attempts to improve labour relations were supported by the unions. Mr. Errol McLeod, President of the Oilfield's Workers' Trade Union (OWTU) which represents TCL workers, recalls that in the past:

Industrial relations was often a response to the attitude of management that labour was not an important consideration. The OWTU was always cognisant of global changes and their impact on the economy. Therefore there is need not just to change machinery but also to change the approach to those who drive the machinery. (...) The relationship between management and union has now changed from an adversarial to a collaborative one, for instance, when TCL decided to establish plants in Jamaica and Barbados it was with the prior consultation and approval of the union. (McLeod, presentation at Caribbean Enterprise Forum, 2001.)

This new approach to labour management has already brought tangible results:

- negotiations in 1997 and 2000 were completed within three months with no work stoppages or third-party intervention
- plant availability and efficiency have increased
- overall cement productivity has increased
- absenteeism has gone down

Equally important, employee satisfaction has improved dramatically (see table 4).

TCL managers summarized the lessons they have learned in figure 1 (Bertrand and McLeod, joint presentation at the Caribbean Enterprise Forum, 2001).

The following case concerning Alcan shows how a tripartite model of workplace governance, which includes a role for government, can improve company competitiveness.

Case 5. Alcan Jamaica Limited: Collective bargaining combined with tripartism[32]

Alcan Jamaica Ltd. is a division of Alcan Aluminum in Canada, which has operated in Jamaica since 1943. The company is a joint venture between the Government of Jamaica and Alcan. It competes in the international market and is therefore exposed to globalization. There are three important challenges for Alcan:

- the price of aluminum has been declining in real terms for over 20 years;
- labour productivity in Jamaica is low by international standards;
- aluminum production in Jamaica has been flat for a while.

As a result of these challenges Alcan Jamaica started to lose its competitive edge. In order to improve the situation, Government, unions and employers have decided to work together. As a first step, a Memorandum of Understanding (MOU) was signed after a three-day retreat attended by the Prime Minister and the Minister of Labour, management and worker representatives. The MOU is a framework agreement for industrial relations which is designed to foster cooperation and inject new life into an ailing industry.

According to the MOU, all three parties commit to:

- cooperative efforts to achieve mutual benefits;
- establishing channels of communication and information sharing between management, workers and Government;
- developing and introducing productivity schemes.

In addition:

- unions commit to refrain from union rivalry and accept the introduction of productivity schemes;
- Government commits to grant tax incentives for productivity schemes;

[32] Based on the joint presentation of Mr. Rickert Allen, Manager, Compensation and Employee Relations and Mr. Norman Da Costa, Vice President and Deputy Island Supervisor, National Workers' Union, Jamaica, at the Caribbean Enterprise Forum, 2001.

Figure 1. TLC: Lessons learned

I. The new vision:

- Recognize the need to change
- Accept responsibilities for change
- Declare and document values in new mission and vision statement that are people-driven and focused
- Communicate, even broadcast, new values

⇩

II. The collective commitment:

- Obtain untainted feedback from workforce and trade union (employee satisfaction survey)
- Resist the automatic response of defence and blame
- Be at risk and encourage positive criticism
- View the process as a never-ending journey and a new way of living
- Religiously monitor and manage the process

⇩

III. Empowered action:

- Jointly develop and implement focused strategies for change
- Treat failures as temporary setbacks to learn from
- Live by your word and speak powerfully
- Recognize and reward change behaviours
- Don't stand on principles that are no longer useful
- Celebrate each successful step in the process

⇩

IV. Desired change

Source: Bertrand and McLeod, joint presentation at the Caribbean Enterprise Forum, 2001

- management commits to more openness and sharing information with its partners – Government and workers.

The MOU was developed in the face of resistance to change due to: managers' fears that their positions were threatened; workers' and union suspicions about the social consequences of the productivity schemes; and initial government reluctance to grant tax cuts. It took some time to open the lines of communication and develop mutual trust. But the MOU eventually delivered results, as one can see from the following evidence:

- recent labour negotiations were completed within the designated time-frame, without any third-party intervention;
- Alcan Jamaica achieved three years of record production;
- productivity has increased by over 25 per cent;
- the cost of production has been reduced;
- the highest sector earnings were recorded;
- capital inflows have increased;
- due to the economic success of Alcan Jamaica, its workers' quality of life has improved, and more social problems of the local community are being addressed.

Moreover, the MOU has changed the culture of industrial relations from adversarial to cooperative. Alcan's success has helped to improve the economy more generally, and other sectors have adopted this valuable tripartite framework of industrial relations.

The next case shows how successful collective bargaining could be the starting point of a large-scale corporate restructuring process.

Case 6. St. Vincent Electricity Company (VINLEC): Enterprise turnaround through collective bargaining[33]

The St. Vincent Electricity Company (VINLEC) is a government-owned electricity monopoly. In the early 1980s it had low population coverage (50 per cent) and highly unreliable service characterized by capacity shortage and load shedding, poor power quality and low safety, and poor system efficiency with 28 per cent losses. VINLEC's poor financial situation with consistent operating losses, negative cash flow, and perpetual overdraft, made it difficult for the company to obtain credit or to finance investment. This situation, combined with inefficient management and a poor company image, caused

[33] Based on the joint presentation made at the Caribbean Enterprise Forum by Mr. Joel Huggins, CEO, VINLEC, and Mr. Noel Jackson, General Secretary, National Workers Union, St. Vincent and the Grenadines.

understaffing at all levels, inadequate training, relatively low wages with few benefits, very low morale, and little organizational commitment. In general, VINLEC was not an attractive company to work for.

The labour relations situation was not much better. The union had only minority support and was thought by a lot of workers to collude with management. The workforce was deeply divided and unhappy.

Over time, the financial situation of VINLEC worsened. The company badly needed money to invest in new capacities, expand services, and improve operations in order to win customer confidence. The only way to attract the needed investment was to build up a good quality and highly motivated workforce.

As a starting point of this transformation, VINLEC decided to improve collective bargaining. The allegedly corrupt incumbent union was out, and recognition was given to the challenger, the National Workers Movement (NWM), which at that time started to enjoy majority support. Once this was done, management and union started to establish an objective basis for collaboration, and a Recognition Agreement was developed. This document proclaimed that:

> The spirit and intention of this Agreement is to maintain and further good relations between the Employer and its Employees represented by the Union, and to provide procedures for the avoidance and settlement of disputes. (…) This Agreement is also intended to promote economical and efficient operation of the works of the Employer, avoid industrial disturbances, achieve the highest level of Employee performance consistent with safety, good health and sustained effort and, to those ends, the Union and the Employer shall together negotiate. (…) On its part, the Employer undertakes to provide good quality jobs in a safe and pleasant environment, and to promote the health, welfare and general satisfaction of all its Employees.

The Recognition Agreement also contained a number of special provisions, such as the basis for recognition, the inalienable rights and responsibilities of employers and unions, mechanisms for dealing with grievances and representations, and the conciliation and arbitration procedures. It specially confirmed the right of workers to union participation. The Agreement also included the corporate mission statement which specifies the company's values. So by signing this Agreement management and the union committed to comply with corporate principles. This made the agreement much more than just an industrial relations document; it became a starting point for corporate restructuring, intended to promote efficiency and high performance levels.

The Recognition Agreement was signed in 1983. Within two years the NWM membership jumped from 60 to 80 per cent. Thereafter management and the union together were able to establish benefits that gave the workers new motivation and improved the situation. Workers became integrally involved in the decision-making process and worker confidence rose. In return, when the company was in the red in 1985, workers agreed to forgo a wage increase. The years 1985–2000 were named “The Period of Consolidation and Confidence Building”.

By 2001 VINLEC had become an extremely successful company and it is now an attractive employer due to:

- its apprenticeship and educational assistance programmes;
- company-sponsored training, including tertiary and professional training;
- scholarships for children;
- medical/health insurance, covering all the family members;
- accident insurance;
- generous pension plan and special retirement considerations for older workers;
- survivor benefits;
- employee loans/advances programme;
- wage policy based on the premise “Pay the best we can afford and sustain”:

  —VINLEC workers are among the 5 per cent best paid in the country;
  —VINLEC has equitable pay scales, determined by job evaluation/grading;
  —VINLEC uses merit-based pay, enshrined in the Recognition Agreement: it has a system of wage adjustments based on the results of individual annual performance evaluations;

- its HR department is known for its honesty, openness, prompt attention to issues and trust.

Union–management cooperation is widespread and effective. VINLEC has union–management committees on:

- health and safety;
- apprenticeship development;
- uniforms;
- pension plan trustees;
- special issues (consultative committee).

Worker grievances are dealt with by union representatives. All union delegates at labour negotiations/discussions (except the General Secretary) are company employees. Training and development for delegates is sponsored by the company. Supervisory staff at VINLEC emerge from the bargaining unit and from among the delegates. The economic results of this corporate turnaround are impressive:

- coverage has improved by 95 per cent;
- reliability is high;
- power quality has improved;
- system efficiency is high (only 10 per cent losses);
- the company's public image has improved;
- customer satisfaction is high;
- the Government appreciates VINLEC's performance;
- transmission/distribution has improved;
- VINLEC has been consistently profitable over the last 10 years;
- the company has a good cash flow, with a 50 per cent contribution to capital investment in the last 5 years;
- the private sector has expressed interest in buying the company's equity.

VINLEC attributes its success largely to the quality of its collective bargaining and labour relations. It lives in accordance with the mission statement enshrined in its Recognition Agreement:

To deliver an electricity service of the best quality and value to our customers; to satisfy the interests of shareholders and employees; to support sustainable development and contribute towards a high quality of life for our people.

ILS concerning recognition of unions and collective bargaining

The main international standards dealing with the right of workers to form unions are the Freedom of Association and Protection of the Right to Organize Convention, 1948 (No. 87), and the Right to Organize and Collective Bargaining Convention, 1949 (No. 98).

At the level of the enterprise, these standards aim to enable workers to coordinate their efforts in order to strengthen their voice at work. Managers should recognize the right of workers to freely form unions or other organizations, and refrain from any action which could prejudice this right. Managers should respect the right of workers to elect professional trade union leaders who do not work in the enterprise or occupation. And of course, they should not interfere in union activities which take place outside working hours. Furthermore, managers should avoid actions which may undermine the union's credibility with its members, such as pre-empting union communications to its members or giving non-union associations or representatives preferential status in negotiations.

Company policies should not tolerate any form of anti-union discrimination in hiring, promotion, job assignments, employment conditions, transfers or dismissals. NUMMI's policy of joint union–management selection of team leaders is a creative way of ensuring that there is no anti-union discrimination.

ILS encourage managers to support workers' organizations through granting time off, providing meeting facilities, permitting access to various workplaces, and so forth. However, managers should refrain from exerting inappropriate influence affecting the independence of trade unions by, for instance, giving financial support with the object of placing the union under management control or promoting the establishment of other organizations under employer domination. ILS are also designed to protect managers' legitimate business interests by further protecting the right of employers to associate, forbidding acts of interference by either party in the other's establishment, functioning or administration, and by protecting the voluntary nature of collective bargaining. The aim is to develop a spirit of cooperation between management and workers' organizations while maintaining their independence, to achieve a reasonable balance between their interests.

To be sure, managers will find it more challenging in some respects to deal with the strengthened bargaining power a union brings to workers. But they will also find that bargaining with union representatives improves labour–management relations by creating a more equal partnership where decisions have more credibility with workers and responsibility is more easily shared. The motivation this provides for employees can be tremendous. Southwest Airlines provided an excellent example of how a more equal partnership can enhance the bottom line for a company.

An established system of communication and cooperation with unions provides an efficient way to gather information on a range of topics (e.g., the work environment, job satisfaction, potential improvements in productivity). Consultation and negotiation with unions is an easier way to include employees (a key group of stakeholders) in decision-making than consulting workers individually. Through unions, managers can more easily hold workers accountable for carrying out tasks for which they are responsible. And working with unions increases transparency and equitable treatment of workers, which gives management more legitimacy.

ILS covering collective bargaining and dispute settlements seek to ensure more equitable bargaining strength between the parties, and to promote individual harmony. Management should respect the right of workers to bargain collectively. Management may bargain with representatives of unorganized workers only if no representative trade union exists, i.e., management should not try to avoid negotiating with union representatives. In many national industrial relations systems, collective bargaining agents are determined on the basis of their representative status, thus permitting more forms of negotiation than with a single representative organization at the enterprise level. We saw in the case of VINLEC that management decided to bargain only with the most representative workers' organization and refused to negotiate with the discredited incumbent. This move helped VINLEC pave the way to healthy industrial relations.

Management representatives engaged in collective bargaining should have the authority and information to take binding decisions. Subjects that are primarily or essentially related to conditions of employment could be included in the scope of collective bargaining (wages, working time, representation, grievance procedures, disciplinary rules, redundancy procedures, and so on). However, subjects that clearly concern the management and operation of a business may be left to management alone to decide (such as business strategy or production methods). Management should provide unions with the information necessary for bargaining, but retain the right to withhold sensitive information.

Respecting the right to bargain collectively can bring many important benefits. It sets out rules for bargaining and grievances that make labour relations smoother and more predictable. Collective bargaining avoids work stoppages or other manifestations of labour discontent. Joint determination of the scope of collective bargaining clarifies which areas are excluded from collective bargaining, and lends legitimacy to those exclusions. Collective bargaining promotes equal treatment and the perception of fairness. Lastly, by engaging in good faith in collective bargaining, management gets across its message that it takes labour rights seriously, which in turn promotes job satisfaction and employee loyalty.

6.2. Employee participation in the decision-making process

Collective bargaining typically focuses on workplace issues and therefore does not cover all the topics of interest to employees. Important matters such as corporate strategy, product quality or technological process, are generally left out. However, those enterprises that put their people first increasingly recognize that getting employees involved in the decision-making process regarding these and other strategically important issues is beneficial for the organization.

Employee participation certainly pays off. According to a study of the Fortune 1000 companies commissioned by the Association for Quality and Participation and the University of Southern California (USC) School of

Business Administration Centre for Effective Organizations (*HR Magazine*, Dec. 1995, p. 21), satisfaction and performance levels are notably higher at companies that have implemented power-sharing programmes.

Companies with high use of power-sharing programmes (involving 40 to 60 per cent of employees) consistently outperformed companies with low use (20 per cent or less of employees) on a range of measures. For instance, the return on sales among high-use companies was 10.3 per cent compared with 6.3 per cent among low-use firms.

"Four percentage points might not seem like a lot, but these are companies with billions of dollars in sales," says Edward E. Lawler III, director of USC's Centre for Business Effectiveness. "The four-point difference equals millions of profit dollars, and that could be a firm's margin for survival" (ibid.).

The study also found significant differences between low and high users in:

- return on investment, 4.7 per cent vs. 6.9 per cent;
- investment, 9 per cent vs. 14.6 per cent;
- equity, 16.6 per cent vs. 22.8 per cent.

In the next section we present the case of a Slovenian company called Trimo Trebnje. After the break-up of Yugoslavia, a lot of companies in the former Yugoslav republics suffered setbacks due to the collapse of economic ties between newly independent states. However, Trimo was able to survive and even penetrate Western European markets, where it is now one of the leading producers of pre-fabricated buildings.

Trimo was able to combine cost leadership and quality strategies to produce cheaper and higher quality products than its competitors. Company management is certain that this success is largely due to the system of employee involvement that was established at Trimo and that allows the company to benefit fully from its employees' creativity and commitment. The employee involvement programme helped the enterprise to capitalize on employees' suggestions, leading to better product quality and optimal technological processes which cut production costs.

Case 1. Achieving corporate success through an employee involvement programme at Trimo Trebnje[34]

Before Slovenia became independent in 1991, Trimo produced metal elements and equipment made from rustproof metal for the Yugoslav market and some

[34] Source: Zupan, 2001.

Table 5. Trimo performance data (financial data in 1,000 tolars, fixed prices as of 1994)

	1994	1995	1996	1997	1998	1999
Number of employees	565	512	428	405	411	**418**
Revenue per employee	7 481	8 585	10 756	11 259	12 521	**17 534**
Profit per employee	33	58	195	202	235	**539**
Value added per employee	1 588	1 866	2 559	2 608	2 688	**3 600**

Note: The average exchange rate in 1994 of 1 euro = 1.2 US dollars = 152 tolars; value added = revenues – material costs – cost of services – depreciation + (–) value of product inventories.

Third World countries. However, as a result of the economic and political turmoil following the break-up of Yugoslavia, Trimo lost most of its Yugoslav market and had to try to penetrate the more demanding Western European markets. Entry to these markets required higher product quality which, in turn, demanded some fundamental changes in corporate philosophy and values.

Today Trimo is the leading company in Europe for the production of construction panels filled with mineral wool. It is present in 13 countries, most of which are members of the European Union. Trimo is an extremely successful company, as shown in table 5.

Trimo's goal and management principles

The first response to the crisis in the early 1990s was a change in top management. Ms. Tatjana Fink, who took over the position of General Manager with a new management team, immediately realized that no success could be achieved unless the company reviewed its goals and management principles. The company's management formulated a visionary new Trimo goal "To become the leading producer of pre-fabricated buildings in Europe by 2010". Primary emphasis was put on customer satisfaction. A new company motto was put forward: "A satisfied customer brings in the biggest profit". It was further recognized that in order to satisfy customer needs, Trimo had to combine cost leadership and quality strategies, i.e., produce higher quality products at a lower cost. Management realized that this objective could be achieved only if the company tapped the skills and creativity of *all* its employees by stimulating the constant generation of new ideas for improving the quality of Trimo products,[35] and, at the same time, improving technological processes in order to reduce costs and increase efficiency. One of Trimo's core values, stated in corporate documents, emphasizes that: "Employees are the source of energy and ideas for Trimo. All employees contribute to success." Ms. Fink echoes this statement: "People are our key resource. You can buy or make technology and getting capital for good projects is not a problem."

These management principles were immediately communicated to all Trimo employees and the goal was achieved through training, information sharing, and employee involvement. In addition to traditional formal and on-the-job training, Trimo has introduced an extensive training programme aimed at explaining the company goal and management principles. Trimo's trade union representative explains: "Each employee had to know why the changes in his/her work environment were needed and why they were significant. Otherwise [workers] felt they were being forced into accepting some ideas from supervisors, that often looked unreasonable to them."

Intense communication and training, coupled with managers leading by example, made workers understand the importance of changes for the survival of the company and for preserving their jobs. Realization of the new company goals and principles led to a situation where employees requested more training. For example, in 1998 as many as 96 per cent of employees expressed a desire to participate in training programmes. More than half the training is done voluntarily, after regular working hours. Through successful training programmes, Trimo has created a multifunctional workforce: more than half the employees are qualified to work in two or more areas.

Trimo management believes that the fast and open flow of information throughout the organization is a key to success. This is achieved through teamwork, which allows people to share information and ideas. Besides permanent work teams, Trimo also forms some occasional teams comprised of employees from different parts of organization. An important tool for information sharing is the so-called "Trimo Dialogue". This started as part of the annual performance review meeting between a worker and a supervisor. Later it became a policy that allows *any* Trimo employee to set up a meeting with *any other* Trimo employee to discuss *any* work-related issues.

---

[35] Schuler and MacMillan (1984) showed more than 15 years ago that a company can improve quality and efficiency from employee commitment associated with employee involvement programmes aimed at improving product quality. Companies such as Westinghouse Electric Corporation, Warner Gear Division of Borg-Warner Corporation, and the Mass Transportation Authority of Flint, Michigan have achieved high product quality and efficiency using such programmes. In addition to increased quality and efficiency, these companies have experienced fewer grievances, reduced absenteeism and turnover, lower design costs, higher engineering productivity, and fewer costly changes in design cycles.

Table 6. Number of PCI projects and participants from 1996 to 1999

Year	Number of PCI projects	Number of different employees involved in PCI projects
1996	31	86
1997	23	66
1998	51	126
1999	59	202

Source: Trimo Business Report

Trimo's success is grounded in two programmes of employee involvement that exist within the organization – the process of continuous improvement (PCI) and the process of continuous care for property (PCCP).

Process of continuous improvement (PCI)

The PCI project, started in 1995, is based on the following assumption expressed in Trimo's corporate documents: "What is excellent today is not excellent tomorrow, and our job is to make the excellence of tomorrow better than the excellence of today." PCI started as a management attempt to encourage workers to become actively involved in quality and efficiency improvements by giving suggestions and initiating possible process and product improvements. Now PCI is the name of a number of projects that can vary in size and business area. Every employee can and is expected to start a PCI by making a suggestion for improvement to the company management, either personally or through the supervisor or representative. The formal methodology of PCI ensures that every suggestion is recorded and later discussed at a meeting of Trimo's top management team. Each approved suggestion is developed into a project with specific goals, assignments, an action plan and deadlines. The person who proposed the improvement can also suggest a team of workers to be assigned to the project. Such a team usually consists of four to eight people from different organizational units and job positions. A special committee appointed by management assesses all the PCI project results and at the end of the year, the best are rewarded.[36]

As can be seen in table 6, the number of PCI projects and people involved

[36] The reward, however, has only a symbolic value since Trimo's culture implies that creativity and innovation from every employee are a part of company expectations.

are constantly increasing. In 1999 almost half (202 out of 418) of Trimo employees were actively involved in at least one PCI project.

In 1999 alone PCI enabled the company to save an estimated 45 million tolars (about 300,000 euro).

Process of continuous care for property (PCCP)

Each of Trimo's tangible assets (office, equipment, inventory) is assigned to a particular employee, whose responsibility is to keep this asset in the best possible condition. Designated employees carry out regular inspections of 'their' property and are required to submit reports on a regular basis. Their work is inspected every month and reported to top management. The delegation of responsibility for corporate property is a form of employee involvement (empowerment) and aims at achieving higher quality products and enhancing employees' commitment to the organization.

Lessons from Trimo

Why has Trimo succeeded while so many other companies have failed? There are a number of lessons that managers can learn from this case:

1. *Emphasize the contribution of employees*. Trimo's management believes that a company that wants to compete in a constantly changing global market depends heavily on its employees, who need to be highly capable and motivated. To produce high-quality goods at the lowest possible cost, firms need committed employees who are innovative and quick to respond to changes in market demand.
2. *Lead by example*. Top management became personally involved in implementing the changes at Trimo, and was, in many cases, a role model. Ms. Fink is a truly charismatic, transformational leader.
3. *Set a clear vision from the very beginning*. From the first day of restructuring Trimo had a clear objective and knew how to achieve it. Through training, information sharing and employee involvement, top management was able to convince workers that the changes were needed.
4. *Show immediate results*. Trimo management constantly updated all employees on progress in restructuring, through training, information sharing and employee involvement.

Trimo suggests numerous ideas for ways to improve enterprise performance by tapping into the employees' organizational commitment and creativity. However, there are some other policies and practices that managers can use to involve employees in decision-making. The following case shows how a company can involve its employees even in decisions which are traditionally the prerogative of top management alone – the promotion and dismissal of the enterprise managers.

Case 2. PSS World Medical: Employee involvement – Firing the boss

PSS World Medical is a speciality marketer and distributor of medical products to physicians, alternate-site imaging centres, long-term care providers and hospitals through more than 100 service centres throughout the United States and five in Europe. The headquarters are in Jacksonville, Florida. O'Reilly and Pfeffer (2000) reported that at PSS the idea of employee empowerment is taken so seriously that people can actually fire their boss. The company's founder and CEO, Pat Kelly believes that this idea is not so radical: "If leaders can't deliver, the *customers* will fire them." PSS is simply solving this problem sooner with fewer consequences for the bottom line. Also, as Mr. Kelly suggests:

> Your people will fire you anyway. They fire you two ways. One, they don't perform. Two, they quit. So, what we try to do is to provide an environment for our employees and for our leaders to understand that, if employees can fire you, maybe you need to be listening to your employees and taking care of your people (O'Reilly and Pfeffer, 2000).

The process works like this: a team of employees may inform a senior executive that they are unhappy with their leader. The senior executive has to meet with the entire team, without the leader. After some open discussion, the leader is brought in. Regardless of the outcome, there are no sanctions against the 'whistle-blowers'. On the contrary, senior management publicly praises them for bringing the problem out into the open. Mr. Kelly summarizes:

> Eighty per cent of the time, the people don't get fired by their people. It's just more opening up communications. Sometimes, they do get fired. We offer soft landings to those, to go back to the level of what they can do. And many of them come back, (…) 60% of our officers have screwed up somewhere along the line, had to be repositioned back, and they subsequently got moved ahead and were very successful as officers.

The following case shows employee participation in a Latin American company.

Case 3. Natura Company in Brazil

Natura, a cosmetics company in Brazil, has used open communication very effectively. Managers are under an obligation to consult with all sales staff in the field, to consider their ideas and suggestions seriously before making a decision, and to transmit the views of the sales staff to various committees. Shareholder meetings are held every three months and all employees are encouraged to attend and express any concerns. And managers are evaluated both on quarterly sales and on staff retention, to ensure that they give high priority to the interests of their workers. This strategy has paid off. From 1994 to 2000 the company grew more than 500 per cent, with over 1 billion dollars in revenues; it now outsells all its national and international competitors.

ILS concerning employee participation

The main international labour standards in the area of employee participation in decision-making are the Co-operation at the Level of the Undertaking Recommendation (No. 94), adopted in 1952, and the Communications within the Undertaking Recommendation (No. 129), adopted in 1967. The Recommendations seek to establish effective communication channels for areas of common interest not covered by collective bargaining and to provide workers with an opportunity to speak up about their workplace concerns.

The Recommendations encourage consultation through voluntary agreements between management and employees. Management, in consultation with workers' representatives, should adopt an effective communication and consultation policy. This should include providing workers or their representatives with relevant information on a particular issue and listening to their views before taking decisions on matters of major interest, such as layoffs. Managers retain discretion in deciding if information is too sensitive to disclose and in making the final decision, but should take workers' views into account as much as possible. Consultations should not seek to undermine the role of unions in areas reserved for collective bargaining. We saw in the case of Trimo how a firm can put these ideas into practice. A good consultation and communications system provides managers with reliable access to the views of workers. It can contribute directly to the success of other management strategies by providing a mechanism for engaging workers in matters such as streamlining production, increasing productivity, and improving quality. It can boost worker morale and loyalty because it sends a credible signal that workers' views are valued and encourages workers to seek out topics to be addressed. And it makes workplace problem-solving systematic rather than ad hoc, which benefits everyone.

In summary, respecting the rights of workers to organize and bargain collectively, and developing communication and consultation channels are an essential part of any people-centred management strategy, and a key to business success.

LAYOFFS AND DOWNSIZING 7

As we have seen, firms which place the human factor at the centre of their business strategy are much more likely to attract and retain capable, loyal and committed workers. They are also better able to develop the organizational infrastructure to put these workers to best use. Furthermore, a multiskilled workforce and good union–management relations will encourage innovation, increase flexibility, and enable the firm to adjust quickly to market changes. Consequently, managers will need to lay workers off much less often than otherwise. Nonetheless, redundancies may be necessary for reasons beyond management control.

In the past layoffs were due to a slump in demand, with workers generally being rehired as the economy picked up again. Today, however, layoffs are just as likely to be due to downsizing. Downsizing refers to permanent job cuts motivated by an effort to improve operating efficiency, not necessarily because of a decline in business. Downsizing has become much more prevalent since the early 1980s. Globalization and increased domestic competition have put great pressure on managers to cut costs, even at seemingly healthy and profitable firms. Indeed, it is becoming common to witness firms simultaneously downsizing and hiring.

Consequently, the traditional job-for-life implicit agreement between workers and firms has gone, even at managerial level. For instance, a recent survey of large employers conducted by The Conference Board reported that 69 per cent of those companies had abandoned policies of job security for their employees; only 3 per cent said that they still had such policies (The Conference Board, 1997). And a benchmarking study of leading companies conducted by the Corporate Leadership Council found an important change in their expectations about career development as compared to the previous decade. They found that companies were now explicitly planning on managerial jobs lasting an average of three to four years. They expected that the incumbents would leave in that time period, instead of continuing until they retired (Corporate Leadership Council, 1995).

A growing body of research has tested the perception that firms improve their financial performance by downsizing. Abowd, Milkovich and Hannon (1990), Caves et al. (1993), and Worrell, Davidson, and Sharma (1991), all find that, on average, financial performance as measured by stock prices seems to decline following downsizing.[37] At least part of the deterioration in performance can be traced to a wide range of adverse effects on the workforce (see, for example, Brockner, 1992, for surveys). But some studies have found that performance improves after downsizing, under certain circumstances. Worrell et al. (1991) find that firms with restructuring plans as part of their downsizing effort show an improvement in stock prices after downsizing. Cascio, Young, and Morris (1997) examined several different model specifications over a longer time horizon and found some positive relationships between reductions in employment and financial performance, although the relationship was generally negative. A study of the positive effects on performance at General Dynamics suggests that the restructuring of firm operations and management that presumably drove much of that company's improved performance both led to and was facilitated by downsizing (Dial and Murphy, 1995).

The effect of plant closings on financial performance is similarly unclear. Blackwell, Marr and Spivey (1990) observed early on that negative relationships between plant closings and enterprise financial performance may be spurious because such decisions are associated with and difficult to untangle from the overall competitiveness of firms. Gombola and Tsetsekos (1992) find that while plant-closing decisions in general hurt share prices, they do not do so for firms that are financially secure. These results are consistent with the view in the downsizing studies that cuts in struggling firms help identify those firms that are already declining while cuts in more successful firms may proxy efforts to restructure and reposition their operations. Kalra, Henderson, and Walker (1994) similarly find that plant closings may be associated with improved performance when firms are restructuring.

Baily, Bartelsman, and Haltiwanger (1996) take a different approach and examine the effects of job reductions on plant productivity using plant-level data from the US Bureau of the Census. They find a range of results, concluding that "plants that increased employment as well as productivity contributed almost as much to overall productivity growth in the 1980s as the plants that increased productivity at the expense of employment".

---

[37] For similar results, see also DeMeuse and Vanderheiden, 1994; Iqbal and Shetty, 1995; and Gunderson, Verma, and Verma, 1997, for Canadian firms.

While there is not much conclusive evidence that downsizing is healthy for a company's financial performance and productivity, strong evidence does exist concerning the effect of downsizing on workers. Apart from the obvious harm done to those who lose their jobs, Baron and Kreps (1999) point out that:

> [T]he evidence concerning the effects of downsizing is clearest and most consistent regarding employee morale and attitudes. Not surprisingly, the effects here are largely negative, manifested in distrust, demotivation, loss of valued employees, stress, and overwork by the stayers.

An American Management Association study reported that among firms implementing job cuts in the 1990s, HR managers reported these immediate and longer-term effects (American Management Association, 1997):

- 69 per cent reported a decline in employee morale within the first year, with 28 per cent reporting diminished morale persisting even longer;[38]
- 42 per cent reported increased resignations and voluntary departures within the first year, with 27 per cent reporting an increase lasting beyond one year;
- 36 per cent reported increased employee turnover within the first year, with 23 per cent reporting a continued increase in turnover beyond one year;
- 13 per cent reported increased disability claims within the year following the layoff, with 8 per cent reporting a persistent increase in disability claims beyond the first year after the layoffs.

David Noer describes the feelings of layoff survivors through the metaphor of the surviving children (box 2).

So overall, the evidence does not seem to support the notion that downsizing and layoffs improve company performance. Nonetheless, employers often feel they must rely on job cuts in order to respond to changing product markets, what Atkinson termed "numerical flexibility" (see Atkinson, 1984).

A variation of numerical flexibility which aims to provide greater employment security is the "core–periphery" model of management (Dyer, Foltman and Milkovich, 1985). Core workers are those whose skills and abilities are crucial to the organization and difficult to replace and so are important to protect. Periphery workers are considered by management to carry out functions that are less crucial to the organization. Necessary adjustments are borne by the periphery, who are often temporary and contract workers. For example, Hewlett Packard outsources less critical work to maintain stable employment. This strategy has some advantages over a pure numerical flexibility approach which exposes the entire staff to greater risk of job loss. Yet it is not without its critics. There has been a lot of debate in Europe (Hakim, 1990) and

---

[38] The morale of survivors suffers most when the layoffs appear to be handled arbitrarily (Brockner, 1992).

Box 2. The metaphor of the surviving children

Think of a family: a father, a mother, and four children, two girls and two boys. The family has been together for a long time, living in a loving, nurturing, trusting environment. The parents take care of the children who reciprocate by being good and fitting in.

Every morning the family has breakfast together. This is a ritual that is similar to an organizational staff meeting. One morning, the children sense that something is wrong. After a painful silence the mother speaks. "Father and I have been reviewing the family budget," she says, avoiding eye contact and staring at her plate. "As you know we are on a fixed income and the cost of food, clothing, and rent are going up faster than our salary. We are no longer subsidized by the government ..." She pauses, then looks at each of the four children in turn. "We just don't have the funds to make ends meet in this new economy," she continues. "As much as we'd like to, we simply can't afford to feed, clothe, and house all four of you." After a painful silence, she points to a boy and a girl, "The two of you must go," she blurts out!

"Don't take it personally," explains the father as he passes out a sheet of paper to each of the children. "As you can see by the numbers in front of you, it is simply an economic decision – we really have no other choice." He continues, forcing a smile, "Don't worry, we have arranged for your aunt and uncle to help you get settled, to aid in your transition."

The next morning, the two remaining children are greeted by a table on which only four places have been set. Two chairs have been removed. All physical evidence of the other two children has vanished. The emotional evidence is suppressed and ignored. No one talks about the two who have disappeared. The parents emphasize to the two remaining children that they should be grateful, "Since, after all, you've been allowed to remain in the family." To show their gratitude the two remaining children will be expected to work harder on the family chores. The father explains that "the work load remains the same even though there are two less of you". The mother reassures them, "This will make us a closer family. You'll need to work harder to help the family survive!"

"Eat your breakfast, children," entreats the father. "After all, food costs money!"

Here are five questions to think about with your colleagues in regard to the story:

What were the children who left feeling? Most managers and leaders come up with words like "anger', "fear", "hurt", and "sadness".

What were the children who remained feeling? Most conclude that the children who remain have the same feelings as those who left. Many often report that the remaining children experience these feelings with more intensity than those who leave.

What were the parents feeling? Although many managers struggle with this question, they often discover that the parents – metaphorically those who remain to manage organizations after downsizing – feel the same emotions as the surviving children.

How different are these feelings from those of survivors in your organization? After honest reflection, many admit that there are striking and alarming similarities.

How productive is a workforce with these survivor feelings? Most conclude that these feelings are a major barrier to productivity.

Source: Noer, 2001.

especially the United Kingdom, where the contingent workforce is of significant size and has clearly been growing (Hunter et al., 1993). Issues include: How does a manager determine which workers are "core" and which "periphery"? Who is responsible for the social protection of the "periphery" workers? And what obligations does the enterprise have with respect to dismissed periphery workers?

Other approaches for responding to change avoid these dilemmas by substituting "functional flexibility" for numerical flexibility. Functional flexibility enables a firm to respond more rapidly and become more competitive in its product market without having to lay workers off. For instance, some European firms have made employees responsible for reaching decisions and taking action themselves without being directed by management (Piore and Sabel, 1984).

Some employers avoid the costly process of layoff by relying instead on attrition to reduce their workforce. Internal labour market arrangements such as internal promotion accomplish much the same thing. Although at least part of the decision to pursue these practices was based on values, particularly the personal values of the company founders, employers also found some advantages from these practices in that they helped maintain loyalty and employee commitment and helped keep together a cohesive employee group ready to plunge into work when business picked up (see, for example, Jacoby, 1985).

Employment security fosters a virtuous circle. Using functional flexibility to avoid layoffs cultivates a stronger commitment from employees and a willingness to innovate and adapt work systems. This permits the smooth introduction of more flexible production methods to improve competitiveness, such as less rigid work schedules.

Empirical studies from many countries around the world, including Finland (Penn, Lilja and Scattergood, 1992), Canada (Grenier, Giles and Bélanger, 1997), South Africa (Horwitz, 1995), Singapore (Sharna and Luh, 1994), Germany, Japan, France (Lorenz, 1992), and the United Kingdom[39] generally illustrate that employers have successfully adjusted to new market situations by using work systems based on functional flexibility that avoid layoffs. The studies look at manufacturing industry where continuous change in product markets requires innovations to existing products rather than entirely new paradigms; for example, car buyers want more variety and more frequent changes in model, but they still want cars as we know them. Innovations in existing products are examples of the type of change that can best be accommodated by a flexible workforce of experienced employees.

[39] In the United Kingdom, the empirical debate over the extent of functional versus numerical flexibility has been particularly intense. See Hunter et al., 1993, for a survey of the debate.

However, even a system of functional flexibility cannot always prevent layoffs. Nonetheless, unavoidable layoffs can be carried out in a way that shows respect for workers and minimizes the negative impact on the firm, as the following cases show.

Case 1. Levi Strauss

Levi Strauss has a commitment to its employees that dates back to the Great American Depression. "Rather than laying off Levi workers, Walter Haas Sr., CEO at the time, put employees on short work weeks, and paid them to lay new floors at the Valencia Street plant in San Francisco until demand for products recovered" (Davenport, 2000). When the firm went public in 1971, its offering prospectus "made corporate history by warning that profits might be affected by a commitment to social programs" (Munk, 1999, cited in O'Reilly and Pfeffer, 2000). Years later, in the 1980s, when the market declined, Levi's did its best to keep its employees or, at least, to provide those being laid off with a cushion. In 1987 Levi's came up with the Levi Strauss Mission and Aspirations Statement. Robert Haas, then CEO, was constantly stating that the company's values and culture are "the glue that unites us, the beacon that guides our action" (ibid.).

In the late 1980s and early 1990s the clothing market improved. Between 1985, when the company went private in a leveraged buyout, and 1996, after the company went public again, the company's stock climbed from US$2.53 to US$265 a share, an increase of more than 10,000 percent. However, in the fall of 1997 Levi announced that it had to close 11 plants in the United States and that approximately 6,400 American employees would be laid off (Verespej, 1998). According to Davenport, "in spite of making the tough downsizing decision, the company's compassion and generosity remained steadfast, with a US$200 million severance package" (Davenport, 2000). Michael Verespej, senior editor for *Industry Week*, describes the package:

> Each laid-off employee received up to three weeks' severance pay for each year of service, eight months' pay from the date of the announcement, outplacement and career-counselling services. What's more, workers were given the entire severance package even if they immediately found new jobs. Levi Strauss also provided company-paid health-care benefits for up to 18 months and up to $6,000 per worker for education, job training, and/or moving expenses.

Levi worked closely with the unions in developing the severance package. Union officials described it as the richest severance package ever offered in the apparel industry. Davenport (2000) cited the statement of Executive Vice President, Bruce Raynor, of the Union of Needletrades, Industrial and Textile

Employees (UNITE), who commented: "The bottom line is that workers still lose their jobs and we regret that, but I think the company really stepped up here and did everything [it] could, within reason, to soften the blow" (Hill, 1998).

Although the union encouraged Levi to cut back its offshore sourcing, union leaders acknowledged that they were pleased that Levi made a commitment to retain 55 per cent of its production in the United States and Canada (Davenport, 2000). In order to save jobs in North America, Levi is implementing gain sharing and teamwork in its American manufacturing facilities in an effort to make them cost competitive so they can stay open (O'Reilly and Pfeffer, 2000). Part of the initiative to change plant operations involved training and sharing more information and decision-making power with line employees. Levi's was one of the early apparel manufacturers to move from a command-and-control system to a more participative management approach.

A lot of enterprise managers claim to care about workers who are laid off. However, not all of them translate this concern into practice. The following case describes a company that indeed is doing a lot for its retrenched employees (ILO, 2001i). As in the case of Levi's, the success of this enterprise is due to the fact that its management policies and practices follow logically from its management philosophy.

Case 2. South African Breweries

South African Breweries (SAB), plc, is listed in London as a FTSE 100 organization with beer, beverage, hotel, and gaming interests that span 21 countries across Africa, Asia and Europe. The group also exports products to 45 countries and is currently expanding its global beer interests. The SAB Ltd. operation in South Africa is the largest single country operation, and the basis from which the international interests have grown. The unique competitive capability of SAB in South Africa has translated into an organization whose practices benchmark favourably with the top five brewing companies in the world in all areas of the value chain from manufacturing, sales, and distribution, to support services such as finance, systems, human resources, procurement, and marketing. This is the result of decades of sustained improvement in productivity and economic value added.

For SAB, increased competitiveness is imperative for the company to survive and grow. The quest for world-class performance results in significant organizational restructuring, with consequent job modification or loss. In 1996, SAB and FAWU (Food and Allied Workers' Union) discussed their mutual interests and FAWU's particular concern about employee security and the effects of global competitiveness. This resulted in Project Noah, aimed at developing alternatives for employees who have been retrenched. SAB and FAWU attended a workshop at the headquarters of the International Labour Organization (ILO) in Geneva, Switzerland. These interactions with the ILO, and with business and labour internationally, reinforced the realities of competitiveness and pointed to the need for creative strategies, which focused on the development of small new enterprises as a global priority. A joint statement of intent emerged from this workshop as the rationale and principles for Project Noah.

Essentially, Project Noah establishes centres in cities or towns in South Africa where SAB retrenchments are anticipated. These centres are temporary, with a lifespan of about eight months, and are staffed with contractors who provide administrative, business and psychological support for retrenchees.

Noah neither replaces nor interferes with any SAB/FAWU agreements and industrial relations processes. Management and the union negotiate on retrenchments and severance packages without any involvement from Noah. While SAB funds all the services and support given to retrenchees, there is no longer an employment relationship between these people and SAB or Noah itself. Retrenchees therefore use the Noah services voluntarily, in line with their own individual needs. Noah cannot guarantee employment; it can simply provide optimum support to enable retrenchees to pursue new careers. It recognizes that personal commitment, effort and enterprise are prerequisites for success.

While many obstacles and frustrations do occur, Noah is encouraged by the success it has achieved to date: 161 small, micro and medium-sized businesses have been launched with retrenchees. These businesses cover a range of industries from farming to manufacturing and services, and have been of real value to both the employed and the unemployed in South Africa.

Noah has also established a business incubator, which has the capacity to house and nurture over 20 small enterprises at any given time. As a joint venture with Government, the community, and labour, SAB also initiated a rural micro incubator in the Eastern Cape, which launched more than 100 businesses in nine months.

Levi and SAB are companies that care about and try to protect their workers even when the market is tight. Whether a company is people-oriented because of the values that drive its activities or because it is the latest management fad becomes obvious in times of economic turmoil. The following case looks at the different reactions of two Silicon Valley companies to the plummeting NASDAQ.

Case 3. Two responses to the collapse of the dotcom sector

In early 2000, business and political commentators declared the triumph of information technology and the new economy. The "dotcomers" working in IT had the working world at their feet. Then suddenly by the end of the same year, the "dotcomers" had to learn a new word – "layoff". As Eric Hellweg put it (Hellweg, 2001):

> It's the height of irony that the Internet industry – the same industry that proclaimed its subservience to the employee, the same industry that built itself around human capital and intellectual heft, the same industry that made a cliché out of the phrase 'your company walks out the door every night' – is the very same industry to gracelessly cast aside those employees.

Here are just a couple of the typical sad stories of January 2001 that have already become part of the dotcom industry folklore. These stories show that no one is immune from being treated as disposable (Salon.com, 25 Jan. 2001).

At Listen.com layoffs came right on the heels of steady expansion. "They kept hiring people in editorial as late as November," says one former employee. "Plus, managers were really tough about allowing people to take vacation time over the Christmas holidays." But just after New Year's Day, many Listen.com employees received voicemail messages instructing them to be at the office by 10 a.m. sharp, at which time they would receive an e-mail directing them to one of two rooms for a mandatory meeting. The news was delivered in a straightforward way: "As you know, there has been a restructuring, and you have been affected by it. You have 45 minutes to get out of the building. The boxes are ready for you to pack your stuff up in." Some workers who were late getting back from the vacation arrived at the office to find that they couldn't get in – their key cards had been disabled. Once they eventually got in, they saw that their e-mail had been cut off.

San Francisco-based ComedyWorld.com announced a massive layoff at a meeting that began at 10 a.m. and lasted about 45 minutes, during which nearly the entire staff was let go. Workers were given exactly half an hour to gather their belongings and files before the building was shut at 11.15 a.m. As ex-employees left via the elevator, the security guards checked bags and interrogated them about company laptops and headphones.

These cases are examples of a lose-lose situation. Employees were treated like disposable material, and the employers lost their reputation as a good place to work. Fortunately, not all hi-tech industry employers share the same approach to layoffs, as the next example shows (Hellweg, 2001).

In January 2001 Amazon (AMZN) announced the closure of its customer service centres in Seattle, Washington and McDonough, Georgia, and a layoff of 1,300 workers. However, Amazon behaved differently from the companies mentioned above. It established a US$2.5 million stock fund to be made available to its laid-off workers in 2003. When times get better again and Amazon is scouting around for talent, these people are more likely to consider coming back.

ILS concerning termination of employment

The Termination of Employment Convention, 1982 (No. 158), and Recommendation, 1982 (No. 166), set out provisions for layoffs and downsizing, as well as individual dismissals. They aim to balance the need of workers for employment security with employers' need for flexibility in hiring and firing.

ILS do not attempt to determine when a firm should or should not lay off workers or downsize. That is a business decision, which ultimately must be left to management. However, ILS do encourage managers to pursue a functional flexibility approach. Management should think about its long-term staffing needs and factor in fluctuations in product demand when hiring. And firms should rely more on multiskilling and flexible work assignments to provide flexibility with a minimum of job loss, similar to the approach established by Levi's founder.

Convention No. 158 also encourages management to inform workers if it intends to restructure. There are two important reasons for this. First, workers should be given a chance to be heard through their union or workers' representative. They may be able to suggest an alternative proposal which is acceptable to management, such as voluntary temporary wage cuts or reduced working time. Second, advance notice gives workers more time to look for a new job and to prepare for possible unemployment. As we saw in the ComedyWorld.com example, a notice period of 45 minutes was unnecessarily insulting, and will certainly not be quickly forgotten by prospective recruits.

Managers are encouraged to offer severance benefits. These should be provided in addition to (or in the absence of) unemployment benefits or a pension, and generally linked to years of service, as at Amazon. Additional measures are certainly encouraged, such as continued medical coverage, as at Levi. Generous severance packages are all the more important if firms follow a core–periphery strategy where a smaller group of workers bears the brunt of layoffs.

Retrenched workers should be given priority in rehiring. This benefits not only the workers, who may find it difficult to get a new job, but also the firm, which saves in recruitment and training costs. Giving preference in hiring to retrenched workers also discourages managers from shortsightedly laying off senior staff and replacing them with inexperienced but cheaper workers, at great cost to the firm's productivity and reputation, as well as to the morale of the remaining employees.

Managers should consider how they can assist retrenched workers to find a job elsewhere. Providing time off while the worker is still employed can be a great help, since it is much easier to find a job when employed than when unemployed. Managers are also encouraged to help retrenched workers in other ways, such as providing training and job search assistance. South African Brewery's Project Noah is a particularly good example of how management can help its former employees.

Lastly, it is critical for managers to ensure that there is no discrimination or retaliation in selecting the workers to be retrenched. Dismissal should never be based on any of the following criteria: union membership or serving as an officer, filing a complaint or giving evidence against an employer, race, sex, colour, national extraction, social origin, political opinion, marital or family status, or temporary illness or injury. However, workers falling into one or more of these categories may be selected for dismissal based on other legitimate criteria such as seniority.

Convention No. 158 also provides guidelines on individual dismissals. Employers are expected to need a certain time (a probation period) in which to determine if the employee is suitable for the job and the work environment, without having to justify their decision. Probation should generally be no longer than six months. After the probation period, the worker should be protected from arbitrary dismissal, i.e., dismissal without a valid reason related to the competence or conduct of the worker. Except in case of serious misconduct, workers should be given verbal or written warnings of inadequate work or unacceptable behaviour, and the right to defend themselves. Managers are encouraged to provide severance benefits, at least where no other income support is available to the worker.

Although dismissal is never easy for either workers or management, a well thought-out procedure, which is as considerate and respectful as possible, can minimize the damage. A dismissal policy that is perceived as fair builds employee loyalty and morale, and makes recruitment easier, whereas a harsh dismissal policy may damage a firm's reputation and brand image, harm community relations, and decrease the company's attractiveness as an employer. A fair dismissal policy can reduce the likelihood of costly industri-alaction or legal action against the firm. Furthermore, evidence from a number of countries shows that increased protection from arbitrary dismissal is an essential part of cultivating worker acceptance of the effects of globalization.[40]

[40] See Deakin (2000) for an ILO study on legislative trends in labour market flexibility.

CHILD AND FORCED LABOUR 8

Most observers would say that using child and forced labour is wrong. But suppose employers can reduce labour costs dramatically by hiring child and forced labour. Can we argue that it is still not in their interest to do so? Consider the following:

To evaluate your (mine, society's) demands for standards, consider two T-shirts, identical in quality and with the same cool logo. One was manufactured by … political prisoners in a labour camp … sexually harassed women in a free trade zone on a Caribbean island … Chinese convict labour … Indonesians whose efforts to unionize are suppressed by army brutality … Americans in a sweat-shop in New York or North Carolina or Los Angeles … whatever grabs you the most. The other was manufactured by Americans … Indians … Malaysians … Costa Ricans … Canadians … Dominicans … Chinese – name your favourite group – working under normal conditions with … an independent union, whose employers treat them as human beings under "reasonable" standards, and whose government protects their basic human rights. The products are the same. The price is the same. Which would you buy?

Now, the vendor raises the price. The T-shirt produced by workers under better standards costs … 50 cents, $1.00, $2.00 – fill in the number – more than the T-shirt produced under poorer standards. Which would you buy? At the same price, most consumers would choose the shirt made under better working conditions. Most would pay a modest premium for that shirt. But as the premium rises, the number willing to do so will fall. This gives us the demand curve for labour standards – the additional amount consumers would pay for products made under "decent conditions".

If this example does not convince you that there is genuine consumer demand for labour standards, consider slavery. Announce that the cheaper shirt is made by slave labour, and see what happens: sales will fall; stores carrying slave-produced products will be boycotted, and so on. In biblical days, in ancient Greece, in the early days of the United States, slavery may have been an acceptable form of labour arrangement. But no longer. Most, if not all of us, do not want to be part of a market transaction where the commodity is produced by slave labour, and would pay to avoid such.

Society can best obtain the standards it wants through a mixture of legal regulation and consumer information, with some standards more efficiently established through the latter and some through the former. Standards governing how the market works, such as those regulating labour contracts and guaranteeing freedom of association, may be more efficaciously set by legal regulations, whereas standards for actual market outcomes, such as wages and hours or occupational health and safety conditions, may possibly be more efficaciously determined through providing consumers with information about those outcomes. (Freeman, 1994.)

The evidence supports Freeman's idea about the importance for a company of consumer demand for labour standards. Several European studies have shown that almost 90 per cent of consumers are more likely to buy a product associated with a good cause, other things being equal. A similar American survey found that more than three quarters of consumers would be likely to switch to brands and/or retailers associated with a good cause and would be prepared to pay a dollar more on a US$20 item for a guarantee that it came from a worker-friendly supplier (*CSR Magazine*, 1999; *Financial Times*, 1999).

A company's performance increasingly depends on its capacity to anticipate and adjust not only to competition and rapid technological transformation, accelerated by the introduction and spread of the Internet, but also by changes in the attitudes of consumers, employees, governments, investors and other stakeholders. Stakeholders expect more from a corporation than just a good product or service. They increasingly choose companies that demonstrate concern for the environment and the communities in which they operate.

The moral desires expressed by various groups of stakeholders are embodied in capital, consumer, and labour markets. Marketplace participants constantly make trade-offs between their moral desires and their desire for lower-priced goods, better investment returns, and so on. The aggregate product of participants' moral desires in their choices as consumers, investors, and employees results in the "morality of markets" and has a significant impact on the outcome of the marketplace. Examples of marketplace morality include investors choosing socially screened investment funds, consumers purchasing dolphin-safe tuna, and employees' desire to work for socially responsible companies.

Based on a social contracts analysis, Wharton Business School Professor Thomas Dunfee has argued that the existence of morality within markets creates certain obligations for corporate management (Dunfee, 1999). These obligations produce four guiding principles:

1. There is a presumption that all corporate actions must be undertaken to maximize shareholder wealth.
2. Managers must respond to and anticipate existing and changing marketplace morality relevant to the firm that may have a negative impact on shareholder wealth.

3. The presumption in principle 1 may be rebutted where clear and convincing evidence exists that marketplace morality relevant to the firm would justify a decision that cannot be shown to directly maximize shareholder wealth.
4. Managers must act consistently with universal norms and principles.

Issues such as child labour and forced labour have an impact on corporate performance more through these "morality of markets" mechanisms than through competitive pressure mechanisms. For example, a 1997 French survey found that 71 per cent of consumers would choose a "child-labour-free" product, even if it was more expensive than other alternatives (Garone, 1999).

Companies respond to these concerns by refusing to use child or forced labour and prohibiting their suppliers from doing so. Such systems are not easy to establish and maintain. For example, a recent ILO study reveals that certain global apparel companies complain that some of their suppliers in developing countries have double books and, at recruitment, some workers use fake passports, which are relatively easy to obtain in many countries (Bodwell and Rogovsky, forthcoming). Many MNEs punish suppliers if underage workers are found there. In some cases, use of underage labour can be a sufficient condition for a multinational to pull out of the factory. In those cases, however, when the multinational opts to stay, it makes factory management terminate the employment of the underage workers, and also pay for their education (ibid.).

Education, rather than exploitation, of young workers is a principle driving serious efforts on the part of MNEs, and also enterprises in the developing countries. This point is illustrated with the following case.

Case 1. Pranda Jewellery public company limited, Thailand[41]

Pranda is one of the prominent Thai manufacturers and exporters of fine gems and jewellery. From a modest beginning in 1973, Pranda now has ten subsidiaries covering Europe, North America, and Asia. Sales amounted to 1,741,219,202 baht (about US$40 million) in 1999 and 2,243,385,612 baht (about US$51 million) in 2000. According to the company's visionary executive chairman Mr. Prida Tiasuwan, success factors have to do with both the quality of Pranda's products and the people who make them.

[41] The information was collected by Nikolai Rogovsky and Fabrice Leclercq of the ILO during their mission to Thailand. The authors would like to express their gratitude to the Employers' Confederation of Thailand, for their valuable assistance.

The Pranda group is a prominent employee champion because of the way it treats its workers. The group overcame the recent Asian crisis without any layoffs. Voluntary turnover is 1.5 per cent a year, which is hardly noticeable in a company with 1,500 employees. Among other prestigious awards, Pranda has been granted a Best Employer Certificate by the Women and Child Labour Inspection Department of Thailand for its stand against child labour. Pranda has not adopted the widespread practice in the jewellery business of hiring workers as young as 12 years of age. In an interview with one of the authors, Pranda's executive chairman, Mr. Prayoon Talerngsri said that the company believes that nobody under 15, which is the legal working age in Thailand, should be hired. Moreover, young employees start with a long and rewarding process of training. Each year Pranda trains over 100 young people, who then become company workers if they choose. Box 3 gives an outline of two programmes for younger workers, most of whom come from poor rural families.

Box 3. Pranda's training programmes

1. **Programmes:**

- Vocational training in cooperation with the Royal Goldsmith College, an institute under the supervision of the Department of Vocational Education, Ministry of Education
- Jewellery-making career development in cooperation with the Department of Labour Skill Development, Ministry of Labour and Social Welfare

2. **Admission qualifications:** People aged 15–22 years, mainly from rural areas
3. **Course duration:** 1.5–3 years
4. **Admission fees:** No fee
5. **Methods of training and development:**

- Principles of jewellery making
- On-the-job training
- Group activities

6. **Conditions for trainees:**

- Free accommodation
- Free meals
- Free medical care
- Social welfare, according to the law
- Free training materials
- Allowance (stipend)

The following case illustrates how a clothing distributor and a manufacturer teamed up to tackle some of the complex issues related to child labour and forced labour.

Case 2. Mabrouc/Prem Group partnership in India[42]

The Prem Group is an Indian manufacturer–exporter which supplies exclusively for Mabrouc SA. The Prem Group started in 1984 as a 100 per cent cotton garment stitching factory located in Tirupur (Tamil Nadu), with a production capacity of 0.5 million units per year and a workforce of 100 employees. Stimulated by Mabrouc, which requires all its suppliers to be SA 8000 certified ("SA" stands for "Social Accountability"), and eager to respond to growing concerns about social accountability, Prem Group went for certification. SA 8000 certification requires, among other things, compliance with ILO labour standards on the minimum age for work *(http://www.sa-intl.org)*. In the process, the company realized that the standards required for certification could only be met through greater control of upstream activities, which led to vertical integration. Today, Prem Group is composed of companies specialized in cotton churning and spinning, knitting, dyeing, cutting and stitching, embroidery and printing. It is thus fully integrated at the production level, with the exception of raw material, since it does not own the cotton fields. Production was first intended solely for export to the Swiss and German markets. Since 1999, Prem Group also supplies Mabrouc with products for the Indian market, which is growing steadily.

Child labour

Prem Group has set the minimum age for recruitment at 18, for all tasks. To implement such standards, systematic checking of young workers' age is necessary. This is done by asking for birth certificates, local school records, passports, and by conducting medical and past events memorization checks. Upon hiring, identity cards are issued and checked afterwards by security personnel. Contractors/suppliers are requested to implement the same principles and to provide a written commitment to that effect.

Prem Group has always implemented these standards. It has no experience of child labour and therefore no story to tell about how to go from child labour to non-child labour. However, if an underage employee were found to be working in the factory, despite the checks mentioned above, it would be

[42] Source: ILO, 2001j.

reported immediately to the personnel manager. For employees between 15 and 18 the company may try to maintain a light workload for a few hours a day (no overtime), combined with school enrolment. For a child under 15, the company will provide free schooling and may pay a stipend to the child to replace lost income to the family.

B.K. Prakash, Prem Group's General Manager and Social Accountability Representative (SAR), insists that "child labour is not only illegal, it spoils the working conditions of a company: although it may seem to make good economic sense in the short term by cutting production costs". He adds, "It has pernicious effects: it discourages education, which hinders human resource development; by way of consequence, it prevents the development of the company due to a lack of mature and educated workers". "From a market point of view," says D. Rufenacht, Head of Environment and Social Relations at Switcher,[43] "Child labour is a time bomb. Recent widely publicized reports on 'children sweatshops' in Pakistan and Bangladesh were highly detrimental to the involved firms' reputation. Companies must come to realize that beyond morality, it makes good economic sense not to take that risk."

In complying with SA 8000 standards, by early 2001 Prem Group had put in place a complete set of social accountability procedures. The company's Social Accountability Systems Policy is well known and widely spread: the policy statement is distributed to workers in their native language (Tamil), to active NGOs and to local and regional political authorities. Several recent press articles have helped diffuse it to the public.

The partnership also established a charitable trust to provide free health, safety and education services to the workers, their families and the public in general. Seven schools are running (ten are planned by end 2002), fully funded by the trust, free of charge for workers' children and other children from poor families. Over 1,200 pupils are now registered. A criterion for selection is the family's motivation to see their children through school. Representatives of Prem Group meet with the families to determine their motivation. Through schooling, the company sees that children who are too young to work are not left on the streets.

Forced labour

Forced labour still exists in many forms, including slavery and abductions, compulsory participation in public works, bonded labour, coercive or deceitful recruitment practices, trafficking in persons, and forced labour in prisons.

[43] Mabrouc's two main brands are Switcher and Whale.

Some businesses knowingly use forced labour. For example, in the United States there was a recent case of women workers from Thailand who were incarcerated in a clandestine garment factory, surrounded by high walls topped by razor wire and patrolled around the clock by guards. The fruits of their work went to pay off "debts". The perpetrators received prison sentences of up to seven years, and were ordered to pay the victims US$4.5 million in compensation (ILO, 2001j).

Of course, the vast majority of employers consider the use of forced labour to be morally repugnant and would not knowingly participate in such degrading treatment of human beings. In fact, many employers and employers' organizations have been very active in adopting codes of conduct for their suppliers, raising awareness and working towards eradicating forced labour. Nonetheless, it is not easy to ensure that an entire supply chain is free from coercion, intimidation, or any other restriction on workers' ability to freely choose their employment.

For instance, an ILO study found that several coercive practices are still commonly used. Some enterprises take workers' passports and refuse to give them back until the end of the contract, so that they are forced to stay and work (ibid.). Middlemen frequently demand recruitment fees on the basis of a cash advance, and prevent a worker from leaving before the advance is paid off. A regional manufacturing manager for Asia of one of the global MNEs says:

> For advances and payments to middlemen, we would consider that [something to consider with regard to] forced labour issues. And we can find this out. We would encourage companies to handle more of their own recruitment.

What is Prem Group doing to fight forced labour? In compliance with the Indian Bonded Labour System Act of 1976, Prem Group does not engage in practices which lead to forced labour: it does not retain personal identification documents, qualification certificates, money deposits and does not support long-term loans, which could prevent workers from leaving the company. Workers are not forced to do overtime, as specified in the labour union agreement. "It is important that workers understand their rights", says P.K. Prakash, "and this can be achieved through good communication: disclosing terms and conditions of work prior to recruitment, making sure that all contracts are fully communicated and fully understood, conducting education programmes to make workers fully aware of their rights and obligations."

ILS concerning child and forced labour

The main ILO Conventions concerning forced and child labour are: the Forced

Labour Convention, 1930 (No. 29), the Abolition of Forced Labour Convention, 1957 (No. 105), the Minimum Age Convention, 1973 (No. 138), and the Worst Forms of Child Labour Convention, 1999 (No. 182).

The main aim of these Conventions is to eliminate the most blatant violations of fundamental human rights. Forced labour (including abduction, bonded labour and indentured servitude) violates the fundamental principle of liberty and human dignity. Child labour robs a young person of the chance to obtain an education and to choose an occupation later in life. The worst forms of child labour threaten the child's life, physical development, and/or moral well-being.

Firms should adopt a clear policy to not use or support child or forced labour in any form, and take adequate steps to ensure that no products of child or forced labour are included in any part of their supply chain.

The minimum age to work in an enterprise should generally be set at no less than 15 years of age, and 18 for arduous or dangerous work, or work that endangers the physical or moral well-being of the young person. As mentioned above, it is not always easy for managers to know the true age of young workers desperate to find a job. They may use fake identity cards, and other workers may collude in deceiving the manager. Therefore, it is important for managers to work with local child welfare organizations and schools, which can verify the age of workers and otherwise help firms develop creative schemes to ensure that young people get an education and are well prepared for work when they reach working age.

Examples of situations which constitute or could lead to forced labour include:

- workers who are physically detained and forced to work;
- workers who are blackmailed into remaining at work – they or their families are threatened with violence, deportation, or such like;
- workers who are not allowed to quit until they pay off a debt, or face any other restrictions on quitting, such as requiring the consent of the supervisor;
- workers who are tricked into believing they must continue to work, such as illiterate workers who have signed a contract which they are made to believe obliges them to continue working even when they would like to leave.

Workers and supervisors at all levels should be trained to ensure that the importance of the policy is well understood and that violations are detected and not tolerated.

Managers should implement a rigorous inspection system to ensure that the policy is adhered to. Important features of a credible inspection system include:

- independence – the monitors should not be linked in any way to the firm or subcontractors, such as depending on them for fees or business referrals. Reputable NGOs and social auditors who work for an association rather than a firm are the best choice;
- non-interference – inspections should be unannounced and unescorted, with independent translation if needed, and anonymity for the workers interviewed;
- whistle-blower protection – there should be a system for receiving information at any time from workers and the community. It should be easy to access, anonymous, not intimidating, and protect the informer from any reprisals. Protection is extremely important because organized crime syndicates are often involved in child and forced labour.

Serious penalties should be clearly announced and strictly adhered to, including loss of job or contract. And the firm should cooperate with the authorities in any criminal proceedings.

Firms should review any practices which may indirectly contribute to child labour. These may include the payment of extremely low wages for subcontracted piecework performed at home, which creates strong incentives for parents to rely on child labour. Firms may also wish to participate in voluntary labelling schemes. Lastly, to the extent possible, firms should take proactive steps to assist the community in combating child labour, such as funding schools and supporting organizations which combat forced labour and trafficking in people.

Purging a firm's goods and services of all forms of child and forced labour is first and foremost a moral issue. Firms must do their utmost to respect these fundamental human rights. But failing to do so is also a poor business strategy. Public knowledge that child or forced labour was used in manufacturing a product can be detrimental to the reputation of a firm and destroy a brand. Quality and productivity can suffer greatly when child or slave labour is used in inputs, as this jeopardizes the quality of the final output. And workforce pride in the final product may be greatly diminished by the knowledge that inputs were produced by child or forced labour, reducing worker loyalty to the firm.

CONCLUSION

The main conclusion of this book is straightforward: decent treatment of workers pays off! Company employees should not be thought of as a cost but as a corporate investment. Superior labour relations and human resource practices can be a valuable source of competitive advantage. International labour standards can help managers to develop the goals and principles they need to achieve this competitive edge.

Yet misconceptions of ILS still abound, and many companies have been slow to see the business advantages of a people-centred business strategy. Instead, they cling to the outdated us-versus-them model of management with its associated labour disputes and work stoppages, loss of efficiency and potential synergies, and general stagnation.

At the same time, several studies indicate that more and more companies realize their competitiveness can be improved through treating their employees with dignity. The cases highlighted above show how enterprises have achieved success by pursuing people-oriented management policies and practices. There are a number of studies using a larger sample over a longer period of time which also show a correlation between such practices and business success:

- A study by Mark Huselid at Rutgers University was based on 968 responses to a survey of the senior human resource professionals in a sample of 3,452 American firms, representing all major industries (Huselid, 1995). Huselid looked at the correlation between high performance work practices and firm performance, controlling for causality. He was able to show that management practices drive performance rather than the other way around. This is an important point. While quite a few observers argue that "if a company is doing all right, it can afford to be nice to its employees", Huselid shows that these companies are doing all right *because* they are nice to their employees. "The magnitude of the returns on investment in high performance work practices is substantial. A one standard deviation increase[44] in such practices is associated with a (...) 7.05 per cent decrease in turnover and, on a per employee basis, US$27,044 more in sales and US$18,641 and US$3,841 more in market value and profits, respectively" (ibid., cited in Pfeffer, 1998).

- Another study by Huselid and Becker shows that for the average firm, a 35 per cent improvement in high performance systems is associated with an increase in shareholder value of more than 20 per cent, or, given the characteristics of the sample, an increase in shareholder wealth of US$41,000 per employee (Huselid and Becker, 1997). Pfeffer's analysis of this finding shows that "since average stock market value per worker for all of the firms in the sample was about US$300,000, firms in the upper 16 per cent of the distribution in terms of their use of high performance management practices experienced about a 14 per cent market value premium – clearly economically substantial" (Pfeffer, 1998).
- In the United Kingdom, the organization that promotes the main employee relations "quality assurance" system, Investors in People (IIP), has argued that companies adopting IIP outperform the national average on a range of financial measures. IIP average return on capital employed is 18.93 per cent, compared with 9.38 per cent national average; pre-tax profit margin is 4.67 per cent, compared with 3.03 per cent national average; sales per employee are GBP£122,108 (US$177,000), compared with GBP£77,447 (US$111,000) national average (RSA Inquiry, 1995).
- *Fortune* magazine reports that 61 publicly traded companies on Fortune's list of "100 Best Companies to Work for in America" posted five-year annual gains of 27.5 per cent, compared with 17.3 per cent for the Russell 3000, an index of companies that mirrors Fortune's 100. Ten-year gains show similar results: 23.4 per cent versus 14.8 per cent. This shows a strong correlation between achieving superior corporate social performance in terms of compensation, benefits, flexibility, and career paths, and achieving better financial performance (Grant, 1998).
- Theresa Welbourne and Alice Andrews demonstrated the causal effect of people-oriented management practices on performance, measured by the five-year survival rate of 136 non-financial companies that initiated their public offerings in the American stock market in 1988 (Welbourne and Andrews, 1996). By 1993, 81 firms, or 60 per cent of the sample, were still in existence. Welbourne and Andrews developed a Human Resource Value Scale, which measures the value the firm places on human resources. A

[44] This represents a 33 per cent improvement.

company's score on this scale was significantly related to the probability of the firm's survival. The difference in survival probability for firms one standard deviation above and one standard deviation below the mean (in the upper 16 per cent and the lower 16 per cent of all firms in the sample) on the human resource value scale was almost 20 per cent.

There are numerous industry studies that show a causal relationship between people-oriented management practices and enterprise performance. Some conclusive evidence comes from a global study of the automobile industry (MacDuffie, 1995; Pil and MacDuffie, 1996), a study of the steel industry (Ichniowski, Shaw and Prennushi, 1994), research on the garment manufacturing industry (Bailey, 1993), a study of the semiconductor manufacturing industry (Brown, 1994), and a number of other industry studies.

We have seen some examples of what enterprises can do to benefit fully from the skills and attitudes of the employees. These successful enterprises attribute their success largely to their people. Not surprisingly, most of these companies do not emphasize financial rewards as means of attracting, retaining and motivating their employees. Research shows quite conclusively that in many cases money is not the most powerful motivator. For instance, according to a recent McKinsey (Chambers et al., 1998) survey of senior managers from a number of well-known companies, having being asked what make them join, stay, or leave the company, out of 5,679 respondents, 58 per cent cited values and culture as being absolutely essential, 56 per cent mentioned freedom and autonomy, 50 per cent – good management, 38 per cent – challenge, and only 23 per cent cited high compensation. The companies described in the previous chapters do not motivate with money. Instead they create and maintain people-centred values and practices, and motivate by giving employees what they really want – trust, respect, freedom, autonomy and good management.

These cases are taken from all over the world and from a wide range of industries, including some labour intensive and low paying ones. People are important and must be treated with dignity and respect regardless of whether they are writing software in a comfortable office in the Silicon Valley or stitching shoes on an assembly line in China.

How have the companies that we have described here achieved their success? In analysing some of the cases described in earlier chapters, O'Reilly and Pfeffer (2000) gave the following answer: "Each of these organizations is based on a set of values that energize their people and unleash the intellectual capital potentially available." However, such an answer is not particularly helpful to managers. As O'Reilly and Pfeffer (2000) put it: "Telling a manager that he or she should tap the intellectual capital of the workforce by promulgating energizing values is akin to telling a parachutist whose chute has fallen that birds fly by flapping their wings." A more specific answer is needed. And here is the one that O'Reilly and Pfeffer rightly suggested:

[These] firms (…) turned the typical logic of strategic management on its head. Instead of beginning with a business strategy, aligning the organization with this strategy, and hiring people to fit the organization, they have begun by being absolutely clear about their values and how these values will define their organizations and determine how they run. (…) Values come first.

The values contained in international labour standards – respect, fairness, trust, freedom, equality – are critical. The transferability of good practices, described in this book, depends on whether or not an organization cultivates these basic values. However, having people-oriented values can't guarantee success by itself. The cases discussed show that a number of other conditions are required.

First, senior managers in the organization must not only follow the fashionable path, but also strongly believe in the values they are trying to promote. Management can't declare one thing and do something different. It has to practise what it preaches, and believe in what it says.

Second, management has to make sure that all the employees of the organization understand and share the corporate values that it is promoting.

Third, values should be stable. Each value can be reflected in a number of different management policies and practices, which may change from time to time. But the values themselves must remain unchanged.

Fourth, management policies and practices should be aligned to the fundamental values and follow from them. These policies and practices should be consistent with each other. Only in this case can one talk about a system of management, rather than a set of mutually independent management policies and practices.

Fifth, senior managers should be leaders, not just day-to-day managers. Dealing with fundamental values and translating them into policies and practices requires vision and long-term strategic planning. This can't be achieved if managers are under pressure to produce immediate results rather than long-term outcomes.

Finally, a business case must be made. Business must be economically viable to survive. Make sure that your people-oriented practices are economically sound. An internally consistent set of management policies and practices should be not only a reflection of fundamental values, but also a part of your company business model that makes economic sense.

ANNEX
LIST OF INTERNATIONAL LABOUR STANDARDS REFERRED TO

Conventions

Weekly Rest (Industry) Convention, 1921 (No. 14)
Forced Labour Convention, 1930 (No. 29)
Forty-Hour Week Convention, 1935 (No. 47)
Holidays with Pay Convention, 1936 (No. 52)
Freedom of Association and Protection of the Right to Organize Convention, 1948 (No. 87)
Right to Organize and Collective Bargaining Convention, 1949 (No. 98)
Equal Remuneration Convention, 1951 (No. 100)
Abolition of Forced Labour Convention, 1957 (No. 105)
Weekly Rest (Commerce and Offices) Convention, 1957 (No. 106)
Discrimination (Employment and Occupation) Convention, 1958 (No. 111)
Minimum Age Convention, 1973 (No. 138)
Termination of Employment Convention, 1982 (No. 158)
Vocational Rehabilitation and Employment (Disabled Persons) Convention, 1983 (No. 159)
Worst Forms of Child Labour Convention, 1999 (No. 182)

Recommendations

Holidays with Pay Recommendation, 1936 (No. 47)
Co-operation at the Level of the Undertaking Recommendation, 1952 (No. 94)
Weekly Rest (Commerce and Offices) Recommendation, 1957 (No. 103)
Reduction of Hours of Work Recommendation, 1962 (No. 116)
Communications within the Undertaking Recommendation, 1967 (No. 129)

Termination of Employment Recommendation, 1982 (No. 166)

The full texts of all ILO Conventions and Recommendations are available online at *http://www.ilolex.ilo.ch: 1567/*

BIBLIOGRAPHY

Abowd, J.; Milkovich, G.; Hannon, J.M. 1990. "The effects of human resource management decisions on shareholder value", in *Industrial and Labor Relations Review* (Ithaca, NY), Vol. 43, No. 3, Feb., pp. 203–236.

Adler, P.S. 1993. "The learning bureaucracy: New United Motor Manufacturing, Inc.", in B. Staw and L. Cummings (eds.): *Research in Organizational Behavior* (Greenwich, CT, JAI Press), Vol. 15.

AES. 1997. *Annual Report 1997*, cited in O'Reilly and Pfeffer, 2000.

American Management Association. 1997. *Corporate job creation, job elimination, and downsizing: Summary of key findings* (New York), available online at http://www.amanet.org/research/archives.htm (4 Apr. 2002).

Atkinson, J. 1984. "Manpower strategies for flexible organizations", in *Personnel Management* (London), Vol. 16, No. 8, Aug., pp. 28–32.

Bailey, T. 1993. "Organizational innovation in the apparel industry", in *Industrial Relations* (Berkeley, CA), Vol. 32, No. 1, Winter, pp. 30–49.

Baily, M.; Bartelsman, E.; Haltiwanger, J. 1996. *Downsizing and productivity growth: Myth or reality?*, CES Discussion Paper 94–4 (Washington, DC, US Bureau of the Census), reprinted in D.G. Mayes (ed.): *Sources of productivity growth* (Cambridge, Cambridge University Press), 1996.

Baron, J.; Kreps, D. 1999. *Strategic human resources: Framework for general managers* (New York, John Wiley & Sons).

Barr, A.; Tessler, S. 1998. "Strategies for survival: The software talent shortage", in *InTelligence Magazine*, Mar., available online at http://www.stanford.edu/group/scip/avsgt/strategies0198.pdf (4 Apr. 2002).

Blackwell, D.; Marr, W.; Spivey, M. 1990. "Plant closing decisions and the market value of the firm", in *Journal of Financial Economics* (Amsterdam), Vol. 26, No. 2, Aug., pp. 277–298.

Bodwell, C.; Rogovsky, N. Forthcoming. *Business and decent work – sport footwear sector* (Geneva, ILO).

Brockner, J. 1992. "Managing the effects of layoffs on survivors", in *California Management Review* (Berkeley, CA), No. 34, Winter, pp. 9–28.

Brown, C. (ed.). 1994. *The Competitive Semiconductor Manufacturing Human Resource Project: First Interim Report* (Berkeley, CA, Institute of Industrial Relations).

Cappelli, P. 2001. "On line recruiting: Will it change everything about managing human resources?", in *Harvard Business Review* (Boston, MA), May.

—. Forthcoming. *Managing without commitment.*

Cascio, W.; Young, C.; Morris, J. 1997. "Financial consequences of employment-change decision in major US corporations", in *Academy of Management Journal* (Briarcliff Manor, NY), Vol. 40, No. 2, Oct., pp. 1175–1189.

Caves, R.; Krepps, M.; White, M.; Farber, H. 1993. "Fat: The displacement of nonproduction workers from US manufacturing industries", in *Brookings Papers on Economic Activity* (Washington, DC), No. 2, pp. 227–288.

Chambers, E.; Foulon, M.; Handfield-Jones, H.; Hankin, S.; Michaels III, E. 1998. "The war for talent", in *McKinsey Quarterly*, Vol. 3, No. 6, Aug.

Choudhury, P. 2001. *Managing organisational change* (Berne, Swiss Agency for Development and Cooperation).

Clerc, J.-M. (ed.). 1985. *Introduction to working conditions and environment* (Geneva, ILO).

Coleman, T.S. 1989. "Unemployment behaviour: Evidence from thc CPS work experience survey", in *Journal of Human Resources* (Madison, WI), Vol. 24, No. 1, Winter.

Collins, J. 2001. *Good to great: Why some companies make the leap ... and others don't* (New York, HarperBusiness).

The Conference Board. 1997. "Implementing the new employment compact", in *HR Executive Review* (New York), Vol. 4, No. 4.

Corporate Leadership Council. 1995. *Perfecting labor markets: Redefining the social contract at the world's high performance corporations* (Washington, DC, The Advisory Board).

CSR Magazine. 1999. June issue.

Davenport, K. 2000. "An independent social audit/external assessment of Levi Strauss", citing www.levistrauss.com (4 Apr. 2002), in J. Logsdon, D. Wood, and L. Benson (eds.): *Research in stakeholder theory, 1997–1998: The Sloan Foundation Migrant Project* (Toronto, Clarkson Centre for Business Ethics, University of Toronto), pp. 101–115.

DeMeuse, K.; Vanderheiden, P. 1994. "Announced layoffs: Their effects on corporate financial performance", in *Human Resource Management Journal* (New York), Vol. 33, No. 4, Winter, pp. 509–530.

Deakin, S. 2000. *Termination of employment and the labour flexibility debate: The reception of ILO Convention No. 158 in common law systems* (Cambridge, ESRC Centre for Business Research, University of Cambridge).

Dial, J.; Murphy, K. 1995. "Incentives, downsizing, and value creation at General Dynamics", in *Journal of Financial Economics* (Amsterdam), Vol. 37, No. 3, Mar., pp. 261–314.

DuBrin, A.J. 1997. *Fundamentals of organizational behavior: An applied approach* (Cincinnati, OH, South-Western College Publishing), p. 99.

Dunfee, T. 1999. "Corporate governance in a market with morality", in *Journal of Law and Contemporary Problems* (Duke University Law School), Vol. 62, No. 3, Summer, available online at http://www.law.duke.edu/journals/62LCPDunfee (4 Apr. 2002).

Dyer, L.; Foltman, F.; Milkovich, G. 1985. "Contemporary employment stabilization practices", in T.A. Kochan and T.A. Barocci (eds.): *Human resource management and industrial relations: Text, reading and cases* (Boston, MA, LittleBrown).

The Economist. 2001. "Business and AIDS: The worst way to lose talent", 10–16 Feb., p. 65.

Ferris, G.R.; Rosen, S.D.; Barnum, D.T. (eds.). 1995. *Handbook of human resource management* (Cambridge, MA/Oxford, Blackwell).

Financial Times. 1999. *A Financial Times guide: Responsible business* (London), June.

Fishman, C. 1998. "The war for talent", in *Fast Company*, Aug.

Freeman, R. 1994. "A hard-headed look at labour standards", in W. Sengenberger and D. Campbell (eds.): *International labour standards and economic interdependence* (Geneva, ILO), p. 81.

—; Medoff, J. 1984. *What do unions do?* (New York, Free Press).

Garcia, A.; Romero, S.; von Bullow, M. 1996. *Human resource development in Mexico: Recent policies* (Geneva, ILO).

Garone, S. 1999. *The link between corporate citizenship and financial performance* (New York, Conference Board).

Ghemawat, P. 1986. "Sustainable advantage", in *Harvard Business Review* (Boston, MA), Vol. 64, No. 5, Sep.–Oct., p. 53.

Godsey, K.D. 1996. "Slow climb to new heights", in *Success Magazine*, Oct.

Gombola, M.; Tsetsekos, G. 1992. "Plant closings for financially weak and financially strong firms", in *Quarterly Journal of Business and Economics* (Lincoln), Vol. 31, No. 3, Summer, pp. 69–83.

Grant, L. 1998. "You Inc.: 100 best companies to work for in America – Happy workers, high returns", in *Fortune*, 12 Jan.

Grenier, J.; Giles, A.; Bélanger, J. 1997. "Internal versus external labor flexibility: A two-plant comparison in Canadian manufacturing", in *Relations Industrielles/Industrial Relations* (Quebec), Vol. 52, No. 4, Fall, pp. 683–711.

Griffin, R.W. 1991. "Effects of work redesign on employee perceptions, attitudes, and behaviors: A long-term investigation", in *Academy of Management Journal* (Briarcliff Manor, NY), Vol. 34, No. 2, June, pp. 425–435.

Gunderson, M.; Verma, A.; Verma, S. 1997. "Impact of layoffs announcements on the market value of the firm", in *Relations Industrielles/Industrial Relations* (Quebec), Vol. 52, No. 2, Spring, pp. 364–381.

Hakim, C. 1990. "Core and periphery in employers' workforce strategies: Evidence from the 1987 employers' labour use strategies survey", in *Work, Employment and Society* (Durham), Vol. 4, No. 2, June.

Hellweg, E. 2001. "A tale of two companies", in *Business2.0*, 1 Feb.

Hill, S. 1998. "Levi Strauss shrinks to fit US market", in *Apparel Industry Magazine* (Atlanta, GA), Vol. 59, No. 1, Jan., pp. 32–43.

Hoffer Gittell, J. 2001. "Investing in relationship", in *Harvard Business Review* (Boston, MA), 1 June.

Holzer, H.; Neumark, D. 2000. "Assessing affirmative action", in *Journal of Economic Literature* (Stanford, CA), Vol. 38, No. 3, pp. 483–595.

Horwitz, F. 1995. "Flexible work practices in South Africa: Economic, labour relations and regulatory considerations", in *Industrial Relations Journal* (Oxford), Vol. 26, No. 4, Dec., pp. 257–266.

HR Magazine. 1995. Dec., p. 21.

Hunter, L.; McGregor, A.; MacInnes, J.; Sproull, A. 1993. "The 'flexible firms': Strategy and segmentation", in *British Journal of Industrial Relations* (London), Vol. 31, No. 3, Sep., pp. 383–408.

Huselid, M. 1995. "The impact of human resource management practices on turnover,productivity, and corporate financial performance", in *Academy of Management Journal* (Briarcliff Manor, NY), Vol. 38, No. 3, June, pp. 645–673.

—; Becker, B. 1997. *The impact of high performance work systems, implementation effectiveness, and alignment with strategy on shareholder wealth*, unpublished paper (New Brunswick, NJ, Rutgers University).

Ichniowski, C.; Shaw, K.; Prennushi, G. 1994. "The effect of human resource management practices on productivity: A study of steel finishing lines", in *American Economic Review* (Princeton, NJ), No. 87, pp. 291–313.

ILO. 2000. *Your voice at work*, ILO Global Report (Geneva).

—. 2001a. *Social accountability and performance: The Switcher/Prem Group experience in India*, paper prepared for the ILO by Professor Cestre, HEC Lausanne.

—. 2001b. "The case of pre-employment training at Volvo cars", in *Discrimination is everybody's business* (Geneva).

—. 2001c. *Empowerment and positive engagement: The Eskom response to HIV/AIDS* (Geneva, ILO, New Academy of Business).

—. 2001d. *The B&Q: Being a better employer, neighbour and trading partner* (Geneva, ILO, New Academy of Business).

—. 2001e. http://www.ilo.org/public/english/employment/skills/training/casest/sats.htm (4 Apr. 2002).

—. 2001f. http://www.ilo.org/public/english/employment/skills/training/casest/mandarin.htm (4 Apr. 2002).

—. 2001g. *Human resources development, employment and globalization in the hotel, catering and tourism sector* (Geneva).

—. 2001h. http://www.ilo.org/public/english/employment/skills/training/casest/thorn.htm (4 Apr. 2002).

—. 2001i. http://www.ilo.org/public/english/employment/skills/training/casest/brewery.htm (4 Apr. 2002).

—. 2001j. *Stopping forced labour*, Global report under the follow-up to the ILO Declaration on Fundamental Principles and Rights at Work (Geneva).

Iqbal, Z.; Shetty, S. 1995. "Layoffs, stock price, and financial condition of the firm", in *Journal of Applied Business Research* (Littleton, CO), Vol. 11, No. 2, Spring, pp. 67–72.

Jacoby, S.M. 1985. *Employing bureaucracy: Managers, unions and the transformation of work in American industry, 1900–1945* (New York, Columbia University Press).

Kalra, R.; Henderson, G.; Walker, M. 1994. "Share price reaction to plant closing abbouncements", in *Journal of Economics and Business* (New York), Vol. 46, No. 5, Dec., pp. 381–395.

Kanter, R.M. 1999. "From spare change to real change: The social sector as beta site for business innovation", in *Harvard Business Review* (Boston, MA), May–June, pp. 122–123.

Kogut, B.; Zander, U. 1992. "Knowledge of the firm, combinative capabilities and the replication of technology", in *Organization Science* (Irvine, CA), Vol. 3, No. 3, Aug., pp. 383–397.

Le Roy, M.; Schultz, J. 1995. "Managing the impact of information technology on human resource management", in Ferris et al., 1995.

Lee, D.M.S. 1999. *Knowledge/skill requirements and professional development of IS/OT workforce: A summary of empirical findings from two studies*, paper prepared for the Panel on Workforce Needs in Information Technology, National Academy of Sciences, 9 Dec.

Levander, M. 1990. "Unions adapt to partnership", in *San Jose Mercury News*, 1 May, cited in O'Reilly and Pfeffer, 2000.

Lieber, R. 1996. "Wired for hiring: Microsoft's slick recruiting machine", in *Fortune*, 5 Feb., pp. 123–124.

Linden, D.W.; Upbin, B. 1996. "Boy scouts on a rampage", in *Forbes*, 1 Jan.

Lorenz, E. 1992. "Trust and the flexible firm: International comparisons", in *Industrial Relations* (Berkeley, CA), Vol. 31, No. 3, Fall, pp. 455–473.

MacDuffie, J.-P. 1995. "International trends in work organization in the auto industry: National-level versus company-level perspectives", in K. Wever and L. Turner (eds.): *The comparative political economy of industrial relations* (Madison, WI, Industrial Relations Research Association).

Markowich, M. 1995. "HR's leadership role in the third wave era", in *HR Magazine* (Alexandria, VA), Vol. 40, No. 9, Sep., pp. 92–100.

Marriot, J.W. Jr.; Brown, A. 1997. *The spirit to serve: Marriott's way* (New York, HarperBusiness).

Maucher, H. 1992. *Leadership in action: Tough-minded strategies from the global giant* (New York, McGraw-Hill).

McCracken, D. 2000. "Winning the talent war for women: Sometimes it takes a revolution", in *Harvard Business Review* (Boston, MA), Nov.–Dec., pp. 159–167.

Metropolitan Life, AIDS Research Unit. 2001. Red Ribbon, available at http://www.redribbon.co.za (4 Apr. 2002), cited in Segel and Sprague, 2001.

Munk, N. 1999. "How CEOs trashed a great American brand", in *Fortune*, 12 Apr., p. 86.

New York Times. 1999. "Personal business: From Texas, with love and peanuts", 14 Mar.

Noer, D. 2001. *Relieving survivors' sickness syndrome after restructuring*, paper commissioned by the ILO (Geneva).

NUMMI. 1993. Internal document, cited in O'Reilly and Pfeffer, 2000.

O'Reilly III, C.; Pfeffer, J. 2000. *Hidden values: How great companies achieve extraordinary results with ordinary people* (Boston, MA, Harvard Business School Press).

Ottaway, R. 1995. Age discrimination adjournment debate, House of Commons, Whitehall, London, 23 May.

Penn, R.; Lilja, K.; Scattergood, H. 1992. "Flexibility and employment patterns in the contemporary paper industry: A comparative analysis of mills in Britain and Finland", in *Journal of Industrial Relations* (Oxford), Vol. 23, No. 3, Autumn, pp. 214–223.

Perotin, V.; Robinson, A. 2000. "Employee participation and equal opportunities practices: Productivity effect and potential complementarities", in *British Journal of Industrial Relations* (London), Vol. 38, No. 4, Dec., pp. 557–593.

Pfeffer, J. 1998. *The human equation: Building profits by putting people first* (Boston, MA, Harvard Business School Press).

Pil, F.K.; MacDuffie, P. 1996. "The adoption of high-involvement work practices", in *Industrial Relations* (Berkeley, CA), Vol. 35, No. 3, July, pp. 423–455.

Piore, M.; Sabel, C. 1984. *The second industrial divide: Possibilities for prosperity* (New York, Basic Books).

Productivity Consulting Group, 1999, cited in O'Reilly and Pfeffer, 2000.

Prusak, L.; Cohen, D. 2001. "How to invest in social capital", in *Harvard Business Review* (Boston, MA), June.

Rajasekar, J.; Gupta, V. 2001. *The case of Larsen & Toubro: Dignified workforce makes for dignified enterprise*, case prepared for the GLOBE (Global Leadership and Organizational Behavior Effectiveness Program), 22 Aug.

Rittenhouse, L. 1998. "Roger W. Sant – Visionary internationalist: An interview with the Chairman, AES Corporation", in *Electricity Journal* (New Albany, OH), Vol. 40, Jan.–Feb.

Rogovsky, N. 2000. *Corporate community involvement: A partner for jobs and development in IILS* (Geneva, ILO).

Rosen, S.; Juris, H. 1995. "Juggling on a high wire: The role of the international human resources manager", in Ferris et al., 1995.

RSA Inquiry 1995, cited in Garone, 1999.

Schlesinger, L.; Heskett, J. 1984. "The service-driven service company", in *Harvard Business Review* (Boston, MA), Vol. 69, No. 5, Sep.–Oct., pp. 71–81.

Schuler, R.S.; MacMillan, I.C. 1984. "Gaining competitive advantage through human resource management practices", in *Human Resource Management*, Vol. 23, No. 3, pp. 241–256, reprinted in F. Foulkes: *Strategic Human Resource Management* (Englewood Cliffs, NJ, Prentice-Hall), 1986.

Segel, K.; Sprague C. 2001. *Metropolitan's response to HIV/AIDS*, unpublished paper commissioned by the ILO (Geneva).

Sessa, V.I.; Jackson, S.E.; Rapini, D.T. 1995. "Workforce diversity: The good, the bad, and the reality", in Ferris et al., 1995.

Sharna, B.; Luh, L. 1994. "Labor market flexibilities as HRM strategies: Example of Singapore", in *Journal of Asian Business* (Ann Arbor, MI), Vol. 10, No. 1, pp. 61–77.

Sheley, E. 1995. "Preventing repetitive motion injuries", in *HR Magazine* (Alexandria, VA), Vol. 40, Oct., pp. 57–60.

Slichter, S.; Healy, J.; Livernash, R. 1960. *The impact of collective bargaining on management* (Washington, DC, Brookings Institution), p. 951.

Southwest Airlines: Annual reports, cited in O'Reilly and Pfeffer, 2000.

Stewart, T.A. 1992. "Allied Signal's turnaround blitz", in *Fortune*, 30 Nov.

—. 1997. *Intellectual capital: The new wealth of organizations* (New York, Currency/Doubleday).

UNAIDS. 2000. *South Africa: Epidemiological Fact Sheet on HIV/AIDS and sexually transmitted diseases*, 2000 update, cited in Segel and Sprague, 2001.

Van Niftrik, J. 2000 "AIDS and employer morality in South Africa", in E. Clarke and K. Strachan (eds.): *Everybody's business: The enlightening truth about AIDS* (Cape Town, Metropolitan Group).

Verespej, M. 1998. "How to manage adversity", in *Industry Week* (Cleveland, OH), Vol. 247, No. 2, 19 Jan., pp. 24–25.

Wall Street Research Net. 1999. Quicksource Report, 14 Dec., available online: http://www.wsrn.com/home/dataset/quicksource.html (4 Apr. 2002).

Welbourne, T.; Andrews, A. 1996. "Predicting performance of initial public offering firms: Should HRM be in the equation?", in *Academy of Management Journal* (Briarcliff Manor, NY), Vol. 38, No. 4, Aug., pp. 904–905.

Wetlaufer, S. 1999. "Organizing for empowerment: An interview with AES's Roger Sant and Dennis Bakke", in *Harvard Business Review* (Boston, MA), Vol. 77, No. 1, Jan.–Feb., p. 123.

Williams, K.; O'Reilly III, C. 1998. "Demography and diversity in organizations: A review of 40 years of research", in B. Staw and R. Sutton (eds.): *Research in Organizational Behavior* (Greenwich, CT, JAI Press), Vol. 20.

World Business Council for Sustainable Development (WBCSD). 2000. *Environmental performance and shareholder value* (Geneva).

Worrell, D.; Davidson, W.; Sharma, V. 1991. "Layoff announcements and stockholder wealth", in *Academy of Management Journal* (Briarcliff Manor, NY), Vol. 34, Sep., pp. 662–678.

http://www.iflyswa.com (4 Apr. 2002).

http://www.sa-intl.org (4 Apr. 2002)

http://www.salon.com/tech/feature/2001/01/25/how_the_ax_falls/index.html (4 Apr. 2002).

Zupan, N. 2001. *Achieving company vision through employee involvement: The case of Trimo Trebnje*, unpublished case commissioned by the ILO (Geneva).